JOHN
PAUL
II

JOHN PAUL II

A Man from Krakow

GEORGE BLAZYNSKI

WEIDENFELD AND NICOLSON
LONDON

Weidenfeld and Nicolson Ltd
91 Clapham High Street, London SW4

ISBN 0 297 77639 8

Printed in Great Britain by
Butler & Tanner Ltd, Frome and London

To Teresa, my wife

Contents

Illustrations

Acknowledgements

Any biographical book that involves a new personality of international stature is of necessity a collective effort. The more so in that the book has had to be researched and written in the comparatively short period of just under nine weeks.

I am grateful to Noel Clark, Maurice Latey and Konrad Syrop of the BBC whose comments and publications gave me some fresh ideas and inspiration of a more general nature. My writing was made much easier by the unfailing help in translation of more difficult theological and philosophical texts, by consultation, research assistance and the expert advice of my former BBC colleague Antoni Pospieszalski. 'The Quarry' and 'Marble Floor' have been taken from *The Easter Vigil and Other Poems* by Karol Wojtyla, translated by Jerzy Peterkiewicz (Hutchinson 1979). My gratitude also extends to Kenneth Mackenzie, Boleslaw Taborski and Christopher Nowakowski for the translation of poems and drama extracts. I am most appreciative of the aid given by the BBC in making available to me some of their files; by the RFE Research Department in Munich (including their New York files); the Polish Episcopate and their Press Office; the Krakow weekly *Tygodnik Powszechny*, their editors and staff; the archives of the Jagellonian University in Krakow and the Pontifical University Angelicum in Rome; the Vatican officials and the Metropolitan Curia in Krakow; the Interpress Agency in Warsaw.

This book could not have been written without scores of people of various nationalities, but mostly Poles – in Poland, Italy, Belgium, France, Germany and some other countries – Karol Wojtyla's friends, relations, colleagues, students, teachers and others, both churchmen and laymen who were so willing to speak to me about his life and works. Finally my special grateful thanks to Christopher Nowakowski whose 'corrective' reading of the manuscript, comments, some eye-witness reports, invaluable support and substantial editorial work greatly contributed to the book in its present form. 'Thank you' also to my many friends and colleagues who freely offered their services in a variety of ways, especially to Carol Bartlett who had the unenviable task of typing the manuscript.

However none of those whose suggestions or assistance I have sought are responsible for the book's contents or errors. That responsibility is mine alone.

I
History in the Making

If there is a saint among the cardinals, he is one; if there is competent man among them – he is the one.

a Vatican Curia bishop

A new era in the history of the Papacy began in Rome on 16 October 1978. In Saint Peter's Square there was a continual buzz of excitement as people waited for the white smoke to appear. When it did, clearly and unmistakably white, the 100,000 strong crowd began to roar: 'Bianca! Bianca!' amid the clapping and cheering. Then, as they waited for the name of the new Pope to be announced, the Swiss Guard turned out and marched up and down the centre of the Square to the deep boom-boom of an enormous drum.

A magnificent orange moon rose from behind the Castel Sant' Angelo. The stage was well and truly set among the ancient columns and ruins of Rome. An echo from the days of the Caesars ... The assistants at the conclave emerged from a door high up in the Vatican and crowded on to a balcony above the Pope's apartments waving to the swelling crowds below. The searchlights finally swung to the balcony of St Peter's and the lights in the Hall of Benediction were switched on. White smoke was still billowing from the improvised chimney of the Sistine Chapel when at 6.40 pm Cardinal Felici stepped out on the balcony and intoned in Latin: 'I announce to you a great joy – *Habemus Papam!*'

The crowd gave a roar, then hushed to hear the name.

Maintaining the suspense, Felici drew out the announcement and the syllables of the name: 'Carolum ...'

The people gasped and waited.

Felici went on: '... Cardinalem ... Wojtyla.'

The crowd faltered. 'Who's he?' Italians asked one another.

The cardinal concluded: '... who has taken the name of John Paul.' This gesture of respect to John Paul I, the Pope we never got to know, the smiling Venetian who died after a thirty-three-day reign, redoubled the cheers that were beginning to roll across the stunned crowd. By now everybody seemed to be sure. 'A foreign Pope!' some shouted. '*E il Polacco*' – it's the Pole. The words ricocheted across St Peter's Square. Then the huge crowd realized that the white smoke above them had just swept away centuries of tradition. The conclave had done not merely the unexpected; it had done the unthinkable.

Shortly before his appearance on the balcony Cardinal Wojtyla suffered the private suspense not only of hearing that he had reached the required number of votes, but of being asked the dramatic question whether or not he accepted and then, immediately after giving his acceptance, by what name he wished to be known.

As Wojtyla carried his well-worn travelling bag into his assigned lodgings in the cramped cell No. 91, he probably did not take his own prospects seriously. Just before the conclave a reporter from *Time* magazine had asked him to sit for a photograph. He waved off the request with a smile, saying: 'Don't worry. I am not going to become Pope.' His last act before entering the conclave had been to instruct his Polish hosts in Rome to book him on the first plane to Krakow, without waiting for the installation ceremony of the new Pope.

During the first day of voting on Sunday 15 October, Wojtyla sat reading a quarterly review of Marxist theory as the time-consuming ballot dragged on. 'Don't you think it is sacrilegious to bring Marxist literature into the Sistine Chapel?' joked a fellow cardinal. Wojtyla smiled: 'My conscience is clear.' On Monday morning on the sixth ballot, Wojtyla gained noticeably. He was so visibly shaken by the coalescing forces that his friends feared he might refuse the Papacy. Cardinal Wyszynski, the Primate of Poland, took him aside and reminded him that acceptance is a cardinal's duty. The election came quickly on the second day and eighth ballot.

Then came the decision. Tears appeared in Wojtyla's eyes when they asked him whether he accepted the election. He buried his forehead in his hands, lowered his eyes, and hesitated for so long that several of the weary cardinals feared that he would reject the awesome office.

Wojtyla composed his answer in Latin, saying: 'Knowing the seriousness of these times, realizing the responsibility of this selection, placing my faith in God, for Christ, for the Virgin Mary, the

Mother of God, respecting fully the apostolic constitution of Paul VI which said "He who will be elected as our successor should not refuse the task to which he was called" ... I accept.'

And when he was asked by what name he should be known, Wojtyla paused for another long moment, then in Latin once more the cardinals heard him say: 'Because of my reverence, love and devotion to John Paul and to Paul VI, who has been my inspiration and my strength, I will take the name of John Paul.'

Then the Papal master of ceremonies acting as notary, with two assistant masters acting as witnesses, drew up a document for history concerning the acceptance by the Pontiff and the name taken by him.

When, within the hour, the new Pope appeared on the balcony, again with tears in his eyes, and told the crowds: 'I was afraid to accept this nomination' it was a statement of fact. The crowd gave him a rousing welcome but their happiness turned to euphoria when he addressed them in flawless Italian, with a clear, baritone voice. Breaking with tradition by giving a short talk before his blessing, using 'I' instead of the ceremonial 'we', and with obvious emotion, he said: 'I speak to you in your – no, our – language. If I make a mistake, please correct me.' Cheers welled up from the Square.

On the night after his election the Pope telephoned an old friend – a priest – in Poland and asked: 'How are things in Krakow? I'm calling because I feel a little lonely. I'm sad without my friends ...'

John Paul II declined the coronation, as did his predecessor, and on the morning of Sunday 22 October he was simply installed as the new Pope during a pontifical mass in St Peter's Square, seen by a crowd of over 250,000 and by countless millions of people all over the world, including Poland, who watched the live transmission on television. When he prayed in front of the gathered thousands, when he raised the heavy golden chalice before the omnipresent stare of television cameras, he did so with all the grace and dignity of the humblest parish priest before his congregation. Suddenly, all the majesty – the centuries-old grandeur of the Papacy, with its gold and crowns, robes and red shoes – was gone. In its place one could see the serenity of a man performing that simplest of acts: an act of sacrifice before the altar of his God.

That same serenity was reflected in the faces of the many cardinals as they knelt before their new Pope. What trace was there of envy? Jealousy? Chagrin? Perhaps it would have needed a cynical eye to

3

spot the dark side of men's souls that day, for the kneeling cardinals doing homage did so with all the joy of old friends celebrating a great event in the life of one of their number. And this same feeling spread through the crowds and spanned the world. Where two or twenty were gathered before a television, there John Paul II's inaugural mass brought home an intimate sharing in the essential joy of the day. 'There you have the face of a man who has great inner depth, of a man who lives with God,' an Italian cardinal told me.

Yet few Popes have been fated to be installed in times of greater fear and uncertainty, and there is no reason to suppose that John Paul II's Papacy will bring any less suffering to the world than took place under his 263 predecessors. But he himself is no stranger to suffering, after being a silent spectator of the Nazi decimation of his native land. All suffering either breaks or strengthens a man's faith in God. Few candidates for the Papacy had passed through a better proving ground. Then too, in a world reeling from the sustained thrust of technology, it is perhaps symbolic that during his inauguration ceremony Pope John Paul II's robe should have slipped back to reveal a stainless steel digital wristwatch. Perhaps the material world and the spiritual can yet find a modus vivendi.

Karol Cardinal Wojtyla journeyed to Rome from his archdiocese in Krakow, that ancient Polish city once the seat of Polish kings, and like Saint Peter before him he has come to Rome to stay. He is the 264th Pontiff of the Roman Catholic Church and spiritual father of over 700 million Catholics in every corner of the world. He has emerged as a spiritual leader out of a Communist-ruled country, 'a man from the front line made commander-in-chief' as one archbishop put it. He has become a Pope for the whole world – for Africa, Latin America, Asia and China as well. He is the first Pope from a Slav nation and the first non-Italian elected since 1522, over 455 years ago. His predecessor then was Hadrian VI of Utrecht, whose short, featureless reign remained famous in the annals of the Papacy only because it led to the Italian monopoly of the Holy See. John Paul II therefore became the first 'international' bishop of Rome and Pope. At fifty-eight he is also the youngest Pope to be elected since 1846, when Pius IX came to the throne at fifty-four and reigned for thirty-one years and seven months. John Paul II may yet lead the Catholic Church into the next millennium.

Almost symbolically, the conclave assembled on St Hedwig's day, a patron saint of Poland. The full Polish television coverage of the

4

investiture in Rome raised intense feelings in the country. One can imagine the reaction to seeing the huge power of the Catholic Church unfolding across the screens of the State's TV network, access to which has been continually denied to the Church in Poland. But most significant of all was that there, at the centre of the world's attention, standing totally assured, was their own man, suddenly elevated to the supreme head of the one institution which Poles happily acknowledge dominates their lives.

When John Paul II knelt before his erstwhile senior Cardinal Wyszynski and kissed the Primate's ring, or when he turned to address the Polish people so warmly in their own language, one could guess that there was scarcely a dry eye in all of Poland, as the London *Times* wrote.

In a statement on 17 October the Polish Episcopate announced:

The servant of the Church of Krakow and of all Poland, the Deputy Chairman of the Conference of the Polish Episcopate, has been elected servant of the servants of God. We believe that it is the achievement not only of the Holy Spirit, but also of Holy Mary, the Mother of the Church, and our Lady of Jasna Gora, whom the newly elected Pope loves so much, and we believe that it is the result of the prayers of the entire Polish people who have received this reward for their faith and the vitality of their religion ...

2

The Church in Poland

In a world full of paradoxes, the paradox of Poland is one of the most outstanding. Although the Polish Communist Party has monopolized power, in an overwhelmingly Catholic country its political control glides helplessly over the surface of society. Given that the Polish community has always been difficult to govern, the difficulty of governing against the popular tide becomes formidable. It is like running an engine without oil: it either seizes up completely or explodes. By now the Polish leadership may have realized, however frightening this realization might prove to be, that they have become the centre of one of the anomalies of modern times: a ruling totalitarian Communist Party without a totalitarian State. In this they are almost unique in the socialist camp.

This paradox is particularly fascinating in the context of State–Church relations. Communism, by definition, is atheistic, yet the overwhelming majority of the people are Catholics. Moreover they are Catholics deeply attached to a Church which has maintained a position of power in relation to the temporal authority unique in Eastern Europe. In no other Communist-ruled country, indeed in no other country, is the Church either so strong or so totally identified with national aspirations as to be the natural focus of all forces opposed to Communism. That is why Communism in Poland is so weak. In very few countries, if any, is it possible to see such Christian fervour in prayers, such intensity of feeling, devotion and even adoration. The churches overflow each Sunday and remain crowded with worshippers of both sexes and of all ages, including most Communist Party members, most days and evenings during the week.

For over a thousand years its Church has been the true custodian of Poland's nationhood and preserved the national tradition and identity. It is both powerful and flourishing and is certainly a key force without whose consent Poland cannot effectively be governed. There is scarcely a village in Poland where the priest is not very much the dominant personality of his parish, as well as being mentor, psychiatrist, lawyer, judge, jury and generally the one called upon to decide all questions between heaven and earth. To wipe out the influence of the priesthood in Poland would be a moral, as well as a physical, impossibility. And no Polish government, unless it wished to divorce itself entirely from the will of the nation, could afford to ignore either the demands or the will of the Church.

The Historical Perspective   In 966 the Polish ruler, Mieszko I married a Christian princess from Bohemia and embraced Christianity, thus bringing Poland into the orbit of the Church of Rome and removing the main pretext for German encroachments. During the next two decades he had to fight the Germans on at least three more occasions, and was victorious each time. But an invasion from the east by Vladimir the Great cost Poland one of her border provinces, which was destined to change hands several times over the centuries. Thus in the first thirty years of recorded Polish history the future pattern began to emerge: pressure from the East and the West.

Mieszko's deliberate decision to embrace Western Christianity proved to be the decisive factor in Poland's survival. The choice of Rome rather than Byzantium brought Poland into the mainstream of Western culture and turned her into an exposed outpost of Catholicism on the eastern borders of Central Europe. When Vladimir the Great embraced the Orthodox branch of Christianity, the two strongest Slav nations, Poland and Russia, were set on their different and frequently colliding courses.

Mieszko died in 992 leaving an established country, albeit a vassal state of the Holy Roman Empire, but well on its way to independence. It fell to Mieszko's eldest son and successor, Boleslaw the Brave, to complete the picture and to transform the dream of greatness and complete independence into a reality. Not only did he extend the frontiers of the Polish state eastwards as far as Kiev, but also in the course of a fifteen-year war with the Holy Roman Empire, he penetrated as far as the gates of Magdeburg on one occasion. For the first and last time in her history, Poland was able to defeat a full-scale simultaneous attack from East and West.

Moreover Boleslaw persuaded both the Pope and the Emperor that the time had come to promote the diocese of Gniezno to the

7

status of an archbishopric. This made the Church in Poland independent of the German ecclesiastical hierarchy, putting it into a direct relationship with Rome. To this day Gniezno remains the See of the Primate of Poland. The Pope also agreed to Boleslaw's coronation, which accordingly took place in Gniezno on Christmas Day in 1024. Poland was now a sovereign state. The Poles became a close-knit nation whose earliest history and thousand-year-old traditions are marked by a living, strong, unbroken and deeply-felt link with the See of Rome, to which 'Polonia semper fidelis' has indeed remained ever faithful.

Since then the equation of Pole and Catholic has become the symbol of the separate identity of the nation as distinct from the Germans and Russians, from the Orthodox and Protestant churches, and from all rationalist, reformist and revolutionary movements on the Euro-Asian continent. Poland has regarded itself as the legendary bastion of Christendom and remained almost immune from various European and Russian cross-currents even in periods of political impotence, division and oppression. Not only has the country hardly been influenced by secularism, but Polish Catholicism has adhered so closely to tradition, both theologically and in its pastoral practice, that it has been less open to modern outward-looking trends within the Church than Catholicism in any other European country.

The strong historical identification of the Catholic Church with Polish nationalism is a key factor in Polish history. Poland, that eastern outpost of Western Christianity, defended itself against incursions from the east and thereby defended not only itself but the whole of Christian Western Europe. The battle of Warsaw in the 1919–20 Polish-Bolshevik war, which Lord D'Abernon has described as the 'eighteenth decisive battle in world history', was merely the latest in a series of epic conflicts which have protected 'civilization' from 'barbarism'. The Poles were victorious in 1920 but the battle of Warsaw, far from redeeming an era, did not save so much as a single generation.

The traditional identification of Poles with Catholicism in post-Reformation Europe was enhanced after the partitions of Poland at the end of the eighteenth century, when the Catholic Church played a crucial part in preserving national identity either by direct participation in the nation's struggle or at least by serving as a national rallying point. Along with the entire Polish population it suffered repression by the occupying powers, particularly Russia and Prussia.

During the Second World War and the German occupation, the Church and its hierarchy took an active part in the resistance movement. The Catholic clergy had an excellent record of wartime resistance. Thousands of priests were imprisoned and about a third of the clergy were killed or perished in concentration camps.

To a great extent both Hitler and Stalin helped to give the Church the unique position it now occupies in Polish life. Before the last war, less than two thirds of Poland's citizens belonged to the Catholic Church, but Hitler's massacre of Polish Jews, combined with Stalin's annexation of the eastern provinces with their large Greek Orthodox and Uniate population, raised the proportion of the Catholic population to over ninety-five per cent. Moreover, Hitler's attempt to turn the Poles into a slave race, followed by Stalin's attempt at ruthless Sovietization, restored to the Church that historical identity with the nation which it had first established during the period of partitions.

Post-war Vicissitudes   The Church emerged from the war with an enhanced prestige. And when the Communists took over, with the past in ruins, the old social order destroyed and old ideas discredited, religion was the one unchanging and unchanged beacon for a nation sailing in the turbulent and hostile waters of the Stalinist post-war period. The Church represented a spiritual, historical and patriotic force far stronger than the Communist Party.

Poland thus became the cockpit of confrontation, coexistence and dialogue between Marxism and Catholicism. The head of the Church, seventy-eight-year-old Cardinal Wyszynski, the Primate of Poland, proved to be a very hard bargainer. Uncompromising whenever the interests of the nation and the Church were threatened, the cardinal was at the same time a subtle diplomat who always knew when to cooperate, what to support, what to oppose, and when. He invariably fought on his own territory, never forgetting that his principal weapon lay in the immense prestige of the Church and of its Primate. Nor did he forget that traditionally, during the period between the death of one king and the enthronement of his successor, the Primate of Poland always assumed the supreme functions of the 'interrex'. The knowledge that the nation had been in the Church's hands for a thousand years before Communism has sustained the Church's confidence. When the visitor or tourist goes into the cellars of Poznan Cathedral, for example, and looks at uncovered and faithfully preserved sections of the foundations of the original church built there a thousand years earlier, then compares these with the foundations of the Communist system with its somewhat briefer history, the Church's attitude becomes clear.

The post-war political role of the Church has been shaped by its history. Traditionally, the Church and its hierarchy were not inclined to participate directly in the exercise of power. History had taught them the instability of political regimes. They understood that institutions deeply rooted in society, in its feelings and traditions, were better fitted to survive. Instead of fighting for political power, the Church has concentrated its efforts on strengthening itself institutionally, and on defending the interests of the nation as a whole against any measures by the Communist leadership which endangered traditional and Christian values.

On the other hand, whenever a dangerous situation has arisen, such as during post-war upheavals and riots, the Church has always stood on the side of peace and order. After the Polish bloodless revolution which brought Wladyslaw Gomulka back to power, and at a time when Soviet tanks were crushing the uprising in Hungary in 1956, Cardinal Wyszynski, just released from a three-year internment in a monastery, appealed to his people for a 'greater heroism' than death with glory. This heroism, he said, was called for in times so pregnant with events and so full of anxiety. The Primate had spoken and the nation obeyed. The oldest and the strongest spiritual power in the land joined Gomulka in his effort to save Poland from a holocaust. Together they succeeded.

Again in December 1970, when the workers' revolt overthrew the Communist Party leadership and government, the Primate appealed for calm and moderation, as he did also in January–February 1971 when Edward Gierek, the new Party leader, faced another even more dangerous confrontation with the workers. This was a time when the country was faced once again with danger from the east. After the June 1976 food price riots, which amounted to a rejection of the policies of the Party leadership and forced the government to capitulate within twenty-four hours, the Primate, while defending the workers' rights and protesting against reprisals, appealed for peace and calm. At the same time he warned the government that it must fully respect human rights as guaranteed by the country's Constitution.

On these occasions the Church's policy not only helped the Communist Party leadership but also saved the system from complete disintegration – a course which in itself might have incalculable consequences, given Poland's present geopolitical situation.

The post-war period of Church–State relations was interspersed by persecution, harassments, truce, dialogue, periods of a fragile modus vivendi, and sometimes cooperation. From the Communist point of view the influence of the Church is a danger and a challenge to the whole Marxist concept. It is the only organization beyond Party control, and it is engaged in a fight for the very soul of Poland. In spite of all the administrative harassments, the Church now has not only more followers but more churches, parish priests and bishops, and more seminaries, than ever before. Each diocese retains its own seminary, and so great are the number of aspirants to the priesthood that some have to be turned away. At Lublin the country boasts the only Catholic university in the Communist world. Independent groups of Catholic intellectuals (KIK) openly organize seminars and meetings in Warsaw and other cities; and throughout the country numerous other organizations thrive, such as the Znak group in Krakow, a Catholic pressure group – linked with the Episcopate – whose main activity is publishing. There are even Catholic deputies in the Sejm (Parliament). Religion is taught in eighteen thousand 'catechetic points' outside schools – in churches, chapels, parish houses and private homes – by priests, monks and laymen. There are only eight-hundred-thousand non-Catholics in Poland out of a population of over thirty-four million. Of the whole population, ninety-three per cent have been baptized in the Catholic Church, and that includes most Party members; ninety per cent of the people regard themselves as faithful believers, regularly attending church services.

The Church is therefore the greatest power in a country ruled by the Communist Party, and in this lies both its strength and its weakness. Strength, because the Communists know that they cannot destroy the Church, and dare not challenge it in a head-on clash. Weakness, because by presenting a danger to Communism, by speaking on behalf of the nation as a whole, it confronts the rulers of Poland with the unenviable dilemma of either surrendering or embarking on the long and hopeless task of working for the slow and gradual erosion of the Church. As Cardinal Wyszynski said, the Communist regime fights the Church because the Church is so strong.

The fundamental conflict comes down to the simple fact that there is a struggle for the 'hearts and minds' of the nation, of which both the Church and the Party are determined to be the sole guarantors and sole spokesmen. What matters for the Church, which knows that nothing is less stable nor more historically transient than a political regime, is to see that religion and Church are as firmly and deeply rooted in the masses of the nation as possible. The Communist system is still regarded by the overwhelming majority of Poles as a foreign, imposed, imported product, even if many of the Communist leaders are seen as Polish patriots who are trying to do the best they can in existing circumstances. But the nation is an entity, global and indivisible.

Who, therefore, has the right to speak in the name of the nation, to express its aspirations and to defend its interests? The Primate? Or the leader of the Communist Party? It is not only a question of ideology, for there are two powerful forces here confronting each other. One – the Party, a small minority – is kept in power by Poland's geopolitical position. The other relies on its thousand-year-old tradition, mass following, and immense prestige built up over the centuries. Both sides, while determined not to surrender their positions, know that another confrontation could lead only to deadlock and disaster. They also realize that it is in the interests of each of them and of the nation to keep the temperature of the conflict as low as possible.

The Church–State battles of the last years of the Gomulka era have, with the coming to power of Gierek in December 1970, been replaced by a more subtle interplay of forces. Right from the start there was an immediate contrast with Gomulka. Gierek, whose formative years were spent in the West, is a pragmatist and realist who wanted to improve living standards drastically and to push the country forward on the road towards modernization, technological revolution and dynamic growth. What Gierek desperately needed in 1971 was national stabilization and unity of purpose. He expected people to work harder and to cooperate in building a modern, streamlined, 'socialist' Poland. He is a Communist but he is also a Pole. What he was trying to prove at all times, and particularly in the face of growing scepticism in the country during 1976–9, is that it is possible to be both at once.

Upon assuming the Party leadership, Gierek immediately launched an initiative aimed at a full normalization of relations between State and Church. He realized that the Church was there to stay, and that the unity of the nation and mobilization of all its creative forces were impossible to achieve without the support of the Church. The Episcopate welcomed the Party's announced intention but made it clear that its interest was in a Church–State reconciliation which respected the Church's interests, not in one dictated by the Party. It raised its own institutional demands, while simultaneously making more directly political appeals for full respect of human rights. These the Episcopate listed in detail, seeking thereby to establish the Church as the arbiter of social policies.

Slowly a degree of normalization began to set in, with many outward signs of improvement in Church–State relations. Some of the Church's demands were met, others rejected courteously or discussed, though without practical results. In some parts of the country local Party authorities continued to exert tough and overbearing pressure on priests and believers. At the top of the Party, however, Gierek assured all believers that honesty and good professional qualifications should henceforth determine a person's standing in his place of work, rather than the question of whether he is a convinced Marxist. Gierek also went on public record as saying that they would 'never attempt to minimize the role of the Church' and that 'the Church is a substantial force in Poland which can help maintain moral values common to all people, regardless of faith'. At the same time some other top Party officials lashed out at what they described as the 'reactionary wing of the Episcopate', which was 'the main organized anti-socialist group in our country', or described the Church as 'an enemy which should be annihilated if possible'. It was difficult to assess how much these contradictory declarations by top Party leaders were intended to calm apprehension and ease pressures both within and without the Party.

The Church's reaction was clear-cut. 'The Church,' Cardinal Wyszynski said, 'does not combat the regime in Poland ... We ask one thing only: that in our homeland Christ has His place, and that the Church is respected in its mission and vocation.' The fairly outspoken communiqués of the Episcopate's conferences – the product of full unanimity among the bishops – and the Primate's sermons both raised the outstanding problems over and over again.

Even so there existed a certain harmony of interests between Gierek and Wyszynski which sometimes led them to an unspoken cooperation. Because he put an end to outright confrontation with the Church and introduced changes to improve the living standards of the people, Gierek enjoyed a certain degree of support from the Episcopate in his initial years. Conversely, Wyszynski's interest in the common good of all Poles was recognized by the leadership. Although incidents of State pressure on the Church occasionally flared up, the atmosphere was generally businesslike, and certainly an improvement over the Gomulka years.

In 1973–4 two parallel developments made an impact on Church–State relations in Poland. Following strong Moscow pressure, a reinforcement of Marxist indoctrination and a general tightening of the ideological screw occurred. These moves were in line with similar developments throughout Eastern Europe, as the countries of the bloc prepared to face the challenge of detente and of a closer relationship with the West in the wake of the Helsinki conference. In Poland some sections of the Party felt that while the Soviet bloc was doing everything to strengthen its ideological unity in the face of detente, this was hardly the moment to be making further major concessions to a Church which openly rejected Party ideology. The Polish leadership had also chosen to foster a long-term transformation of Polish society with the double goal of modernizing both economy and society and thereby undermining the traditional strength of the Church. 'Socialization' was the ultimate aim. Thus the Party leadership found itself in a paradoxical situation. On the one hand it desperately needed the Church's support in implementing its socio-economic policies and securing a form of continuous dialogue and understanding with the nation; on the other, after almost three years of relatively pragmatic rule, it began to place an increasing and fruitless stress on ideology. Incentives are as much a part of such a long-term master plan as deterrents.

The Polish leadership's plan to 'socialize' society has been closely related to the position and influence of the Church. While on the one hand concessions, and the quest for normalization and cooperation, were dictated by the facts of political life, the Party itself was trying to outflank the Church and undermine its long-term position without actually confronting the institution as such. In 1974 the

Primate made the Church's position absolutely clear: 'For us, next to God, our first love is Poland. After God one must above all remain faithful to one's homeland, to the Polish national culture. Above all we demand the right to live in accordance with the spirit, history, culture and language of our own Polish land: that same culture which has been used by our ancestors for centuries.'

Fruitful cooperation, as advocated by Gierek, will depend on the assessment by both partners of what lies in the national interest. The Episcopate has been opposing a 'socialization' based on strict Communist doctrine. Whenever Party leaders have tended to over-stress orthodox (and therefore defunct) ideology they have come up against strong opposition from the Church. There has been no such opposition when they thought in terms of some genuine social transformation. When Gierek proposed to modernize the Polish economy and raise the population's standard of living he was fully supported by the Church. But specific programmes such as the socialization of agriculture, the ideologization of the educational system or the undermining of lay Catholic organizations were strongly opposed. Although these measures did not constitute a direct offensive against the Church, each in turn might in the long run weaken its influence within society while expanding the role of the State. For with its powerful Church and mainly private agri-culture, Poland is conspicuously less socialist than its neighbours. The leadership apparently felt that re-ideologization and a strengthening of the 'leading role' of the Communist Party would help to make up for these glaring defects. The sequel to the Episco-pate's natural scepticism about the proposed 'socialization' measures was increasing pressure on the authorities from the Pri-mate to meet increasing Church demands.

All this has made the Polish Church a de facto political opposi-tion. For both political and doctrinal reasons, however, the Episco-pate has sought to avoid giving the impression that it was a political force agitating against the government. Instead it has tried to use its influence to press for measures which would advance both the nation's and the Church's interests, and most of all that respect for civic human rights which is guaranteed by Poland's Constitution. The Church leaders, knowing that there was a time to keep silent and a time to speak out, have used their influence in a highly diplo-matic way, frequently pressing for changes when no real Church–State tensions were evident, and refraining from comment when social strains in the country were at their greatest. Some Catholic politicians have told this author that the Church does not want to be regarded as a fighting or as an oppositional force. The State and the Episcopate should argue, agree, disagree, or even agree to disagree. Sometimes the Church would accept this compromise or even support the Party leader.

As a result of such an approach to crucial problems, the Church can both challenge and support government policy, depending on how it assesses the stability of the situation. The government has sometimes responded to this give-and-take approach, especially in its appeals for unity among Poles regardless of religion, when social tensions have been especially high. The result has been a subtle interplay of Church and State initiatives. But if the Church represents a 'loyal opposition' then it is certainly not loyal to the Party. The Episcopate is uncompromisingly opposed to Marxist–Leninist philosophy. Instead it sees itself as the protector of the country's national interests, the defender of the faith, of the nation, and of citizens' rights.

It is this viewpoint which has led the Episcopate to agree with the government whenever the overriding interests of the Polish nation were concerned. But when the boundaries of strategic necessity are overstepped, or Warsaw seems, for example, to be coming too close to Soviet ideology and practice, then the agreement between Church and State ends. This qualified loyalty of the Church's opposition has been extremely important to the Party leader, and he has indirectly acknowledged it in his speeches. But the Episcopate has also shown that it expects concessions in return for its responsible attitude and that it can switch to the offensive if it feels its demands are not being heeded.

Never since the crisis Christmas of 1970–1 did Gierek so desperately need the Church's support as in the aftermath of the June 1976 food price riots. At the end of an unprecedentedly prosperous five-year period in Poland's post-war history, marked by efforts to establish a personal dialogue with the people, dynamic economic growth and endeavours to simultaneously develop heavy industry and a consumer society, Gierek came up against the brutal constraints of economic reality both in the country and in the world at large. A belated attempt to get the economy back on the rails by a package of huge price increases in June 1976 provoked massive workers' protests, strikes and riots. The unrest forced the leadership to capitulate within twenty-four hours. It was the third capitulation in six years.

The June crisis had been preceded by a series of unnecessary and often provocative government measures and therefore growing social unrest, which showed how much importance people had attached to an agreement on political consultations which they believed that the leadership had finally concluded with them after decades of authoritarian rule. Polish society insisted that the leadership acknowledge the real political meaning of its pledge and that this be put into practice. Gierek's initial success generated what could be described as a revolution of rising expectations. When the crunch came people felt misled, angry and frustrated. For several months the Party outdid itself in contradictory measures, hesitations, inertia and diffidence. The regime was sitting on a powderkeg, managing to unite against itself the Church, workers, peasants, students and intellectuals.

But the government had to face something else as well. From June 1976 onwards more or less loosely organized opposition groups appeared on the scene, embracing intellectuals, academics, students, peasants and workers. They represented all political attitudes from, in Western terms, radical Marxist left to radical and nationalist right. These motley groups acted openly and exerted a dual pressure on the authorities. In their various unofficial and un-censored publications they demanded full respect for human rights and condemned police brutality, reprisals against the workers and harassment of their own activities. But they also launched a series of political and economic programmes, all of them, with one or two exceptions, within the limits of Poland's geopolitical position.

This opposition movement is now stronger, more widespread, active, massive, better organized and more vocal than any other in Eastern Europe – a phenomenon which owes its existence to a wider context of pressure from social groups – and the Church is the foundation on which it rests. The Episcopate has never directly supported the oppositional organizations, but has at all times indirectly condemned the authorities' behaviour towards them and demanded complete freedom of speech, assembly and expression. It has also protested against reprisals and police brutality towards workers, and against harassment of the opposition movements' activists.

From Dialogue to Cooperation? In this climate the single most important political event in 1977 was the summit meeting between Gierek and Cardinal Wyszynski on 29 October. The official communiqué said that Gierek had exchanged views with the Primate on 'the most important problems facing the nation and the Church; problems which are of great significance for the unity of Poles in the work of shaping the prosperity of People's Poland'. The two most powerful men in Poland were talking openly and honestly together.

Both were deeply concerned about the state of the country. Gierek had asked the cardinal and the Church for help in calming the troubled economic waters and slowing down mounting political opposition from below. The situation had become so serious that any minor incident could have far-reaching national consequences. 'We are administering the country,' a highly-placed Party member told me, 'but the cardinal is ruling the nation and the people's souls. He has much greater influence than we could ever hope to have, since he is talking to the nation in terms of timeless national values which appeal to ordinary people.'

Even the most dogmatic Communists have realized by now that the Church is no passing phenomenon. Indeed, Gierek once said privately that it would be here forever, and one member of the Party Central Committee told this author that it would be a catastrophe if there were no powerful Church in Poland today.

The operative word in the Gierek–Wyszynski communiqué was the 'unity' of the nation. The situation in the country was discussed at length by both men, and the Primate defined the Church's position along the lines of the Episcopate's various pastoral letters. No details were discussed at the meeting but some promises were made by Gierek. Both leaders were reported to have agreed that the nation had to brace itself patiently to overcome its difficulties. However the Church insisted that justice must not only be done, but be seen to be done.

Both men were fully aware of the limitations inherent in the present system, but neither the Church nor the people were convinced that the limits either of freedom or of political manœuvre had been fully reached by the Communist Party. In a sermon given a few days later, Cardinal Wyszynski emphasized that in 'especially difficult situations' he must 'clearly see the demands of Polish raison d'état'.

The plain fact that the leader of a Communist, and therefore by definition atheist, Party had asked for help from the Church requires no comment. It is a telling paradox of life in Poland, the more so since it was followed on 1 December 1977 by Gierek's historic audience with Pope Paul VI, the first ever by a ruling Polish Communist Party leader. The Pope said that the Church stood ready today, as in the past, to offer Polish society its cooperation. There were, however, conditions that would make such cooperation more effective: a climate marked by confidence in the relations between Church and State and the recognition of the Church's proper tasks and mission in the modern reality of the country. 'The Church's contribution,' the late Pope said, 'will have a much greater prospect of being effective to the extent that other conditions, starting from the education and upbringing of youth and including the environmental conditions and socio-economic situation of the country and its population, become equally better.'

It soon became clear that the government had tried to obtain the Church's cooperation at a minimal cost to itself and through rather insignificant concessions, even if the Primate was now described by the authorities as 'an eminent Polish patriot'. Official talks and negotiations between the government and the Episcopate were resumed, but no significant results appeared. The bishops expressed the desire to continue them but stressed several times that there could be no normalization of Church–State relations unless they were based on recognition by the authorities of the public and legal character of the Church, as was the case before the war, and on a corresponding bilateral agreement.

The logic of the demand was obvious. The Church has never been recognized as a legal entity in post-war Poland, a factor which of itself has created much difficulty and confusion in such areas as the purchase of property and the signing of contracts. The return of its lost legal status would make the bishops' work essentially easier and more effective. It would mean that they could formally uphold the Church's constitutionally granted rights before the courts; it would give them more freedom in organizational and administrative matters, e.g. in the construction of Church buildings and the supervision of Church agencies and auxiliaries; it would offer more effective protection of the interests of priests and religious workers; and it would lend momentum and authority to the Church's legitimate demands for a more generous measure of religious and human rights.

Archbishop Luigi Poggi, the Vatican's roving ambassador in charge of Polish affairs, reported in the Vatican after his return from Poland in June 1978 that the government was 'not yet ready' to grant full legal rights to the Church. In November 1978, at the beginning of John Paul II's pontificate, I was in Warsaw and discussed the present state of Church–State relations in Poland. It immediately became clear that the situation is far from settled. An official statement handed to me by Kazimierz Kąkol, the minister in charge of the Office of Religious Denominations, described relations as being 'devoid of conflicts and tensions' and heading, particularly in recent years, towards a 'distinct normalization'. This, according to Kakol, does not mean that 'there is no controversy, no difference of opinion, nor is there full agreement on attitudes'. But if there exists 'respect for the overriding values of the good of the nation and of patriotism common to all, these differences could be overcome through consultation and mutual agreement'.

Freedom of conscience and religion and equality under the law are guaranteed by the Polish constitution, which also proclaims the separation of Church and State. The State's policy on religion does not depend on changing conditions. A believer, Kąkol maintained, 'is not faced with the necessity of choosing between his loyalty towards a socialist State and loyalty to his faith'. This policy is based 'on the recognition of values to which, historically, the Church has contributed during the country's development and also on recognition of the positive results of the Church's educational influence in shaping citizens' attitudes today'.

Accepting these premises, Party leader Edward Gierek advanced his thesis on the possibility of cooperation between State and Church in achieving aims important for the nation as a whole. Kąkol emphasized that the process of normalization is two-sided, and is accompanied by the parallel process of normalization in relations between Warsaw and the Vatican. Gierek's audience with Paul VI produced some important statements with regard to relations between State and Church, the role and place of the Church in a Polish 'socialist reality' and 'the tasks of the universal Church vis à vis the problems of the modern world'. The official statement went on to say: 'A constructive practice of mutual relations and a fruitful dialogue which helps to deepen mutual understanding is being con-

tinued – and is based on the fact that the moral-political unity of
the Polish nation is invaluable and that differences of *Weltans-
chauung* should not undermine it.'

So much for the official view. A somewhat different picture
emerges from my talks with the Polish Episcopate and their official
spokesman. Little has changed in practice, I was told. Plenty of soft
words are being used, but with no concrete results to show for it.
While Gierek's intentions might be honourable, he is nevertheless
faced with opposition from within the Party.

The Church's position was frequently and clearly outlined in,
for example, the Episcopate's communiqué of December 1977, the
Primate's Epiphany sermon on 6 January 1978 and at least two
pastoral letters, the latest one in September 1978. The bishops and
Primate came out with some hard-hitting statements condemning
the process of imposed atheization, stressing the dangers of
'socialist' education and demanding full recognition of the public
and legal status of the Church and a corresponding bilateral
agreement.

The Church also referred to a long list of repeated complaints
that the State has thus far failed, or refused, to act upon. These
include restrictions on free public expression, discriminatory
measures against practising Catholics who hold important public
posts, the frequent withholding of authority to build or rebuild
churches (although 385 such authorizations were granted in 1971–
8), the harassment of priests and of people hiring out premises for
religious functions, the lack of social insurance for clergy employed
in Church institutions, and the State's monopoly of student organizations. On the last point the bishops explicitly demanded the creation of an independent Catholic student organization, since, they
said, the groups controlled by the State stand against a Christian
upbringing of the majority of the nation's academic youth and thus
cannot represent their interests.

In a sermon delivered on 6 January 1978, Cardinal Wyszynski
declared the Church hierarchy's willingness and competence to cooperate with the authorities towards forging a moral renewal of the
nation. Among the more urgent steps that had to be taken in this
direction, the cardinal not only sought formal recognition of the
Church as a legal body but also listed in his proposals the re-estab-
lishment of traditional Christian associations and the setting up of
an independent Catholic press. Then the Episcopate once again

raised the problem of the way the nation was being forced into a monolithic, materialistic and secular mould that was utterly alien to the Polish spirit. The restriction of science and research, as well as artistic and religious activity, through State censorship was to be regretted, the bishops said. The Church would accordingly support those initiatives which strove to manifest the culture, the products of the human spirit, and the history of the nation in an authentic form, because the nation had a right to objective truth about itself.

Finally on 17 September 1978 the Episcopate demanded the limitation or even abolition of State censorship, which, it declared, 'has always been and still is a weapon of totalitarian regimes'. Censorship was an institution that crippled the cultural and religious life of the entire nation, and misinformed the people. Millions of believers were being deprived of expression by the limited printing of religious instruction books and journals, and the State's refusal to allow the Church access to radio and television. The official media had instead been 'given over to the service of an ideology aimed at bringing up men without God', and were being 'used to impose just one set of views and models of behaviour on the nation and to wield power over its people'. In a situation where millions of believers were being robbed of access to religious publications the Episcopate called on the State to allow at least one independent Catholic daily, and to permit the mass with its sermon to be broadcast on Sundays and holy days.

The Episcopal letter went on to urge Catholics to develop a critical attitude towards State-monopolized information, to make use of 'other more reliable sources', and to protest whenever the official media offended Christian principles or attacked those unable to answer back. In an apparent reference to Polish dissenters and opposition groups, the letter condemned 'harassment of people who have the courage to openly express their opinion about public affairs and the contents of the official mass media'. The right to freely express one's opinions, the bishops concluded, is a necessity, for 'without freedom, man atrophies, and all progress is condemned to a slow death. We cannot disavow our right to criticism. We demand to be respected and to have our convictions taken in earnest.'

By statements such as those above, the Church has engaged the government on the most important political issue of the day: the ability of a Communist system within the Soviet orbit to allow its citizens freedom of speech, information and debate.

Recognition of the Church's legal status is a precondition to any formal agreements with the State, the Episcopate's spokesman told me in November 1978. The Church would never agree to subordinate its institutions to the existing law on associations. Such a move would be tantamount to signing its own death warrant, because the basic unresolved conflict between the Church and Marxist ideology would remain. Today the authorities have to accept the Church as a reality, but at the same time they impose militant atheism wherever possible.

The whole tenor of the Church's latest statements has strongly demonstrated that it refuses to be swept up by the euphoria that the domestic media attempted to create in the wake of Gierek's audience with Pope Paul VI. The Party First Secretary's repeated assurances that no conflict exists in Church–State relations have been denied and contradicted. What the Episcopate is saying, in fact, is that there *are* conflicts, and that until these are settled to the Church's satisfaction its contribution to surmounting the nation's continuing state of near crisis will be impaired. The partnership being requested by the State must, in other words, be genuine. One of the partners in such a relationship cannot be expected to bear a full share of the burden if it is continually crippled in its functioning; nor, for that matter, can the Polish public to whom the Church will ultimately make its appeal.

Nevertheless, times have changed. Once the Church in Poland was seen as a 'Church of Silence', a victim of Communism perhaps a step away from martyrdom, and thus a cause deserving support. Now the Polish bishops find that when they meet churchmen from other parts of the world attitudes are no longer the same. Now they are being asked – and their interlocutors are usually from countries where Communist regimes are thought to be a distinct possibility in the near future – just how does the Polish Church cope with the country's Communist government?

In his reply to the congratulations sent him by the Polish leadership, John Paul II wrote:

It is our fervent desire that Poland develops both spiritually and materially with peace, justice and a respect for men. In the spirit of the dialogue begun by the great predecessors whose names I bear, I wish, with God's assistance, likewise to do everything useful for the good of my beloved nation, whose history has been linked for a thousand years with the mission and service of the Catholic Church.

Replying to an address of greetings from Cardinal Wyszynski, during an audience given to the Polish bishops and pilgrims in Rome, the Pope paid tribute to the Polish Primate:

There would be no Polish Pope in the Holy See, beginning this new Pontificate full of the fear of God, but also full of confidence in Him, if it were not for your faith, which did not flinch in the face of imprisonment and suffering, and your heroic hopes, your boundless faith in the Mother of the Church ... and the whole period in the history of the Church in our homeland which is linked with your service as bishop and Primate.

3

The Formative Years

His Country and Heritage The baby Wojtyla was born into an infant country barely a year and six months older than himself. For the Polish State, often powerful in history, had been utterly erased from the maps of Europe between 1772 and 1795 in an almost Darwinian example of the demise of the weakest. And it was only on 11 November 1918, when the smoke of war was beginning to clear over most of Europe, that the independence of Poland was proclaimed. The boy born in Wadowice near Krakow on 18 May 1920 belonged to the first generation of free Poles for nearly 150 years.

It is impossible to divorce a man from his background, to study him in isolation without taking into account the subtle interplay of culture, tradition and heritage which all help to shape his outlook and his concept of reality. What sort of country was Poland then, and what sort of people were the Poles in 1920?

Like most newly created states, Poland had an excess of patriotic zeal in lieu of military might or even economic necessities. Only three months after Wojtyla was born, the fledgling Polish state, which was already locked in a fight to the death with the Bolshevik army, now found the enemy at the gates of Warsaw. Here the Poles achieved their greatest triumph. The Red Army was defeated in the historic battle of Warsaw – the so-called 'miracle on the Vistula'. Poland, and incidentally Western Europe, was saved and the war with Soviet Russia ended. Patriotic fervour reached new peaks. The new nation began to build itself with optimism and faith, standing over its legacy of rubble from the 1,750,000 buildings totally destroyed in the First World War.

Poland's faith was in the future, and above all in God and the Virgin Mary, for religion had been the spiritual bread which had kept the Poles alive when oppression was at its cruellest in the nineteenth century. Nevertheless, although Catholicism was the dominant religion in the Polish nation into which Karol Wojtyla was born, it was far from being the only one. In the east, the post-1920 borders included many Orthodox believers. Nearer the west, Lutheran communities existed, while ten per cent of the country's population were Jewish.

Apart from religion, another factor deeply rooted in the Polish soul was the effect on the people's outlook of generations of oppression. In Warsaw, the Citadel which had housed the Russian garrison still had its heavy guns pointing not outwards but inwards, at the heart of the capital. There too stood the Brama Stracen – the execution gate from whose hooks condemned Poles would be hanged and left to struggle for minutes on end until the rope slowly killed them. Like the Russians, so too had the Prussians and the Austrians ruled their respective parts of Poland with an iron hand, though here at least a dim awareness slowly grew about the needs and aspirations of the subject peoples, and in the case of the Austrians many beneficial reforms came over the years.

Religion and oppression were thus the two cornerstones of Polish psychology: the oppression long and bloody, the religion steadfast and unquestioning. Yet perhaps by the time that Karol Wojtyla was born, the people of his parents' generation had the right to feel that now, at last, the sufferings of the past were over.

History was to show that this was no permanent change, only an interlude of barely twenty-one years. Wojtyla in the meanwhile grew up in the traditions of the Polish nation: love of freedom, tolerance, justice, human dignity, and a Christian tradition going back almost a thousand years. He was also born into a country which was, and is, particularly conscious of the price of peace. In his formative years Wojtyla experienced the tragedy and desolation which fell upon Poland during the Second World War, when almost a third of the Polish nation died. He was destined to learn of the horrors of Auschwitz (Oswiecim), so close to his home, and then after the Nazi horror to live under imposed Soviet Communism, yet alongside the growing cohesion and renewal of the Church.

There are four landmarks of human hope and tragedy under whose shadows Wojtyla grew up and worked and they are all to be found within the single archdiocese of Krakow: the shrine of Czestochowa, the gas chambers of Auschwitz, the city of Krakow, and the blast furnaces of Nowa Huta.

Every year hundreds of thousands of Poles make their annual pilgrimage to Czestochowa, on the Warta river. Some come on foot, others by train, bus, lorry or horse-drawn cart. A hundred years ago Czestochowa was no more than a large village with nine thousand inhabitants. Today there are over 160,000 people living in the town to which the large Bierut steelworks have brought new prosperity. The pilgrims flock to the centuries-old Pauline monastery and church standing on the Jasna Gora hill, just outside Czestochowa, with its miraculous image of the Black Madonna. It is Poland's most revered shrine.

The monastery in which the Black Madonna painting is kept is also a fortress which flung back an invading Swedish army in the seventeenth century when both Warsaw and Krakow had been overrun. It was a miraculous victory, after which the Polish king, John Casimir, proclaimed the Madonna to be the Queen of Poland. Henceforth to affirm the cult of Our Lady in Poland was to affirm the Polish spirit. The image of the Madonna is adorned with a cloak covered in military honours, all attesting to battles and wars fought by Poland. To see that picture, which unites Polish national pride with a religious emotion, is to begin to understand Poland today.

On one occasion over a million pilgrims assembled at Czestochowa to attend masses, and to listen to the sermons of Cardinal Wyszynski, the Primate of Poland, and Cardinal Wojtyla. At six in the morning thousands of people both young and old, women and workers in their overalls, attend the first masses. Long queues form before the confessionals. The mass is said in Polish and the Primate delivers the sermon.

In 1973, ten thousand pilgrims marched from Warsaw to Czestochowa. Eighty per cent of them were young people. They sang their kind of songs, played guitars and recited prayers, often written by themselves. The new look of the new generation was well received by the older pilgrims, many of them simple people who said: 'Well, they are different, they are breaking away from our customs, but it's good that they are with us – that we are together.' Karol Wojtyla, first as a young priest, and then later as bishop, archbishop and cardinal, was always there celebrating masses, leading pilgrimages and meeting people. From time to time each year he rode on his bicycle the 140 kilometres from Krakow to Czestochowa with groups of young people – said a monk at Jasna Gora. Sometimes the gate was closed because they arrived late at night, and they had to knock to be let in.

And then too, Wojtyla lived in the shadow of Auschwitz (Oswie-cim), and in fear of forced labour under Nazi rule. Auschwitz, that memorial to millions of gassed Jews, Poles, Russians – all those whom Hitler deemed subhuman in his twisted, hateful ideology.

Lying north-west of Krakow, the death camp stands as the satanic antithesis to Czestochowa. With its barbed wire now rusty and its ovens silent, with its collection of unneeded shoes and other relics, Auschwitz too draws its pilgrims. Many of these are young people, born after Hitler. They do not sing here, nor play guitars, though many pray. Instead they stand and look and try to imagine the unimaginable; think the unthinkable. No man can walk along the disused railway line and under the '*Arbeit macht frei*' sign without returning as if from Golgotha.

It was first as an archbishop and later as a cardinal that Wojtyla led sad pilgrimages of priests and former inmates of Auschwitz to Auschwitz and once to Rome to celebrate the Golden Jubilee of the ordination of Paul VI.

Krakow was Cardinal Wojtyla's capital as the See of the archdiocese. '*Cracovia totius Poloniae urbs celeberrima*' runs an inscription on a sixteenth-century effigy in the city – 'Krakow, Poland's most celebrated city'. The inscription is perhaps as true today as it was when the old city was the capital of the Jagellonian dynasty which linked Poland to Lithuania and transformed it, during a golden age, into one of Europe's foremost powers and the first ever Commonwealth of Nations. For the old order left behind it the rich architecture and tapestries of artists whose names read like the pages of an historical 'Who's Who' of European art. It also left the Jagellonian University, named after King Wladyslaw Jagiello, the second oldest in Central-East Europe, dating back to 1364. Then there are the Wawel Royal Castle on the rock, with its cathedral, and the Mariacki (St Mary's) church on the old Market Place, and many other churches built in bygone centuries to testify to Man's belief in God and to the richness of the human spirit. And beneath the present cathedral can be found other, still older, foundations tracing an historical thread back to the tenth century.

Krakow is at once both the Oxford and Winchester of Poland: its historic seat of learning and its ancient capital. It has also been the custodian of Polish nationalism in the years when the country was parcelled out among Prussia, Russia and Maria Teresa of Austria. Perhaps the tears of compassion which she is reputed to have shed were genuine enough, for those parts of southern Poland which fell under Austrian domination came to enjoy the greatest freedom and self-government, with Krakow as the principal centre of jurisdiction and culture. Here the Polish language could be freely used and Poles could hold public office. Here, in corners of the city such as the Michalik Café, patriots and nationalists dreamed and planned for the day when the whole of Poland would be united. It was thanks to Krakow that Polish literature flourished; its writers and pamphleteers reached out to Poles living in the stern greyness of Prussian Poland or those forced to suffer the tinsel autocracy of the Tsar.

When the Second World War broke out, Krakow was bombed on the first day of the fighting, though by subsequent wartime standards the destruction was light. The ancient city was fully preserved, and after the war the new districts took on the mantle of a modern town complete with streamlined blocks of flats and offices. A whole new post-war generation now looks out over Krakow's stones and frescos, churches and citadels and learns about the times and peoples who inspired them. And, being a university town, Krakow has many young people with young ideas and outlooks; people who have taught themselves to think, to question.

Krakow nourishes such curiosity. To the newcomer it is a city full of the unusual, the odd and the perplexing. Why, for instance, does the Mariacki church have two towers side by side, both utterly different in their construction and in height? Why does the city have so many ancient buildings with façades hiding sloping roofs in a mésalliance of Italian and Northern European styles? Why does an effigy of Christ crucified hanging in the cathedral show Him beardless? Why does a bugler appear on top of the Mariacki church tower at noon each day and begin playing a bugle call which he stops in mid-note? Why are there so many names of Celtic origin in Krakow itself and in the surrounding countryside? And is it true that, according to a Hindu legend, after God had created the world he had still seven stones left; these He threw on the earth and the cities which grew up where they fell will never perish: Rome, Vyšehrad, Krakow, Delhi, Jerusalem, Mecca and Delphi.

Of course, the people of Krakow have answers for all these mysteries, some based on fact, others on legends passed down over the ages so that the truth behind them has been worn down beyond recognition. Indeed the whole place is built on half legend, half truth. They say a fierce dragon – one of many which must have roamed Europe during the Dark Ages – lived in a cave by the Vistula river and annually demanded a young virgin from the local people. A gallant young knight called Krakus slew the dragon, not by the usual frontal attack but by feeding it salt and sulphur-laden sheep. The beast then tried to quench its powerful thirst in the Vistula and burst its bowels from drinking too much water. The grateful people named the town after the hero. There the legend ends. But the fact remains that Wawel Castle and its cathedral, the very heart of Krakow, stand on a hill directly below an empty cave ...

The old Market Place in Krakow, locally known as 'the drawing room', has all the urbane sophistication of a university town meeting place in which ideas and gossip can be exchanged and liberal, progressive people flourish. But Krakow is fiercely rooted in tradition, and whatever Marxist–Catholic dialogues take place at these tables in the Market Place, they are always under the shadow of the Mariacki church tower from which every hour on the hour a bugler sounds a link with the past: the call of the vigilant medieval watchman. The call always stops short at the moment the bugler was struck in the throat by a Tartar arrow in the thirteenth century. Krakow stands firm on history and tradition.

That is why the huge steelworks named after Lenin, and the first 'socialist' new town, Nowa Huta, were built years ago just outside Krakow as a shop window for socialism, meant to temper the religiosity of the city. This was to be a model of progressive socialist planning – wide streets, high-rise flats, but no church: socialist steelworkers do not need religion. But, as subsequent developments showed, it seems they need it more than socialist slogans. On 15 May 1977 thousands of Catholics, workers, soldiers, women and girls, stood patiently in the rain as Nowa Huta's first church was consecrated by Cardinal Wojtyla, after seventeen years of clashes with the authorities over the question of religion.

It was here that in 1960 hundreds of believers, including old women, moved in to protect a single wooden cross which had served as a centre for the town's open-air worship. When police proposed to remove the cross a crowd stoned them. The police replied with tear gas but the cross remained. For several years between four and six thousand workers from the 'socialist town' attended twelve masses held every Sunday in the open air below the cross, often kneeling in the rain, sometimes in the snow, and frequently in the mud. Cardinal Wojtyla celebrated Christmas midnight mass there.

These days, I am told, there are two new plants in Nowa Huta: a new steelworks and a new factory of the 'Holy Ghost' – in other words the new church of Notre Dame, the Queen of Poland. Paradoxically, it stands at the junction of the Karl Marx and Great Proletariat Avenues in Nowa Huta. It is fascinating and, at the same time, unreal to look at this highly modern church, built on three levels and reminiscent in style of the famous churches of the French architect Le Corbusier, against the background of huge steel structures and blast furnaces in the foundry complex. The church itself was built by thousands of volunteers and amateurs, helped by thirty specialists and qualified workers. The granite façade, for instance, was built using two thousand stones which could only be found in one river bed in the countryside. The stones were brought into the town, and polished by young people. Near the church stands a massive steel cross, seventy metres high, a gift from Austria. Within the crypt, in the Chapel of Reconciliation, is a series of moving pietà entitled 'Christ in Auschwitz', executed by a well-known Polish sculptor.

Karol Wojtyla led the seventeen-year-long struggle to build this church. He mustered the labour, money and materials and mobilized so much outrage through petitions and sermons that the authorities began to fear open revolt. And when Cardinal Wojtyla presided triumphantly over the dedication he told a weeping, exulting crowd of over fifty thousand: 'Nowa Huta was built as a city without God. But the will of God and the people who worked here prevailed. Let this be a lesson.'

A Boy Called Lolek The story begins in the study of the parish priest in the little town of Wadowice. Portraits of the Primate of Poland, Cardinal Wyszynski, of Paul VI, and of Cardinal Wojtyla, now John Paul II, decorate the room with its old Polish-style tile stove in the corner. And here also in the cupboard is the register of births for the decade 1917–27. On page 549 the birth of a male, Karol Jozef Wojtyla, to Karol and Emilia née Kaczorowska is duly registered on 18 May 1920. To the parish records, which include a note in Latin about the baptism of Karol, its present parson Fr Zacher has since added: 'On 16 October AD 1978 he was elected to the See of Peter, assuming the name John Paul II.'

Outside the church in a small street an old woman, Mrs P, has a fruit and vegetable stall. Fifty-eight years ago she was a young midwife and delivered the baby Wojtyla into this world. As far as she remembers there were no complications. She used to know the Wojtyla family very well. 'You must have known Lolek?' a waiter in a restaurant asked me. He was shocked that I did not, and that I had only once met Archbishop Wojtyla in Krakow in 1964: everybody seemed to know Lolek (a diminutive of Karol). The older people certainly did; the younger people had heard about him from their parents; and the children learned on the day of his election that the new Pope is really their own Lolek from Wadowice. That is how he was known during his life there, both as a young lad and then as a schoolboy at the local grammar school. Many of his friends call him Lolek or Karol to this very day.

Wadowice is a sleepy little town of fifteen thousand inhabitants about fifty kilometres south-west of Krakow. It is six-hundred years old and situated in the picturesque foothills of the Beskidy mountains (one of the Carpathian range) on the fast-flowing Skawa river, a tributary of the Vistula. Its life revolves around the market place, now called Red Army Square, lined with low buildings on all sides, and with a monument to the Soviet soldiers in the centre. But it is dominated in the south-west corner by the pale brown parish church, with its bulbous copula, dating back to the fourteenth century. Here Lolek was baptized.

On one side of the church is a short street with two old terraced houses painted in contrasting shades of grey and yellow. The second house contained the Wojtyla family flat. You turn a corner, enter a dark courtyard, then pass through a dilapidated door and climb a flight of stone stairs to find yourself on the first-floor iron gangway outside. A door leads straight into the kitchen, and through it to the two rooms which make up the flat. From his corner room Lolek often watched the sundial on the church marking the passing hours.

On the other side of the church in an adjacent street stands a long low building. This was once the primary school to which Lolek went at the age of six and stayed for four years. Today the building houses the local militia headquarters, various political organizations and local authority offices. When, as a ten-year-old boy in 1930, he began his grammar school education, Lolek had only to walk from the church across the square and into a sidestreet to reach his state grammar school, a large two-floor building named after one Maciej Wadowica.

Near the end of November 1978, and many weeks after the election, the new Pope's photographs were still displayed in many windows, while papal white and yellow and Polish national white and red flags fluttered in the late autumn wind all over Wadowice, including the Soviet monument. As one priest said: 'Mr Brezhnev must have been nearly choked by the white smoke from the Sistine Chapel this time.'

The Wojtyla family originated from the village of Czaniec, near Andrychow. Lolek's grandfather Maciej was a tailor and had settled in Biala Krakowska (now part of a provincial capital). The young boy's father Karol lived for a time in Czaniec, where some of his relatives are buried. Recently, when speaking at a local church, Cardinal Wojtyla referred to these men and said with pride that his forefathers led pilgrimages to Calvary, one of the revered shrines in Poland. After Lolek's father had married in Wadowice, apparently he did not take particular pains to maintain contact with his home town, and settled in Wadowice instead. There he served with the 12th Infantry Regiment as a staff officer in an administrative capacity. He retired as a captain of the Polish army (he had served with the Austrian army before Polish Independence) on a rather low pension, even by the standards of the day. Family life was thus far from easy and their circumstances were very modest.

Wojtyla's childhood was not particularly happy, not least because of the difficult conditions of everyday life in the years after the First World War. His mother's health was poor, though she tried to do whatever was best for her baby, and used to push his pram through a neighbour's garden so that the baby could have some fresh air. The neighbour still remembers when Emilia Wojtyla would call up laughing from the garden: 'You will see, my Lolek will grow up to be a great man.' Her parents came from Silesia, so that German was one of the first languages that young Karol learned. When he was four he often travelled up to Krakow with his mother to stay with his godmother and her daughter, who still lives near Krakow's Old Market Place. She was Lolek's first cousin and remembers him as a very kind and unfailingly polite child.

Lolek's mother died from a heart complaint when he was nine. He was at primary school by then, and her death hung over him for a long time. Wojtyla bears an uncanny resemblance to his mother. There is something expressive about seeing these two faces together in a photograph. Four years later his only elder brother,

Edmund, a doctor working in Bielsko, died after contracting scarlet fever. A Mrs S was present when news of the death reached Lolek: 'I noticed him standing alone and sad outside the front gate. In a moment of emotion I took him in my arms and kissed him. "Poor Lolek," I said, "you've lost your brother." The grave-faced thirteen-year-old looked up at me and said simply: "It was God's will." '

So Wojtyla spent his teens living alone with his father. The old man was a tower of strength. Being a professional soldier of iron discipline, he demanded conscientiousness, diligence and obedience from his son. He often left Lolek in an unheated room to strengthen the boy morally and physically. But he was also a warm-hearted father, and a man of culture and of high intellectual standards. He was deeply religious, but free of any bigotry. He ran the household, cooked for Lolek (they often had their meals together at a neighbour's house), washed and mended his clothes. He acted as his son's tutor and coached and coaxed the lad from his first school exercise book through to matriculation. Father and son were inseparable; in the evenings they would go on long walks together, talking and discussing everything and anything.

In the mornings before going to school the young Lolek always stopped off to pray in church. He had a deep sense of religion and was very active at the school's Marian Society (Sodalis Marianus), serving as its president for over three years.

Many people you can speak to in Wadowice knew him in those days, and out of their various memories a picture of the young Wojtyla begins to emerge. In his schoolwork the boy excelled in religious education, Latin, Greek, German and introductory philosophy classes. According to those school reports still in existence he got the highest marks ('Very Good') in all subjects except history, physics and chemistry (he was only 'good' in these). His teacher of Polish recalls his extremely dependable character and undoubted gifts for the humanities: he could fire his friends with enthusiasm for the theatre and was fascinated by his country's language and literature. He helped his weaker classmates with their work both in school and at their homes. In Greek and Latin he was top of the school, and made even his teachers feel uncomfortable sometimes by his grasp and knowledge of the languages. Fr F., who knew Wojtyla as a keen altar boy and got to know him still more intimately through the confessional and through frequent visits to his home, remembers him as a very tall, somewhat chubby boy, very lively, intelligent, quick-witted and extremely well behaved, with a cheerful, optimistic personality. While at grammar school Wojtyla studied the philosophy of Kant, and one of his close former school friends recalls: 'He was streets ahead of us in his general knowledge and in his interests.'

Always intensely loyal to his friends, some of them Jewish, Wojtyla never fell foul of his teachers. Everybody liked him. Among his many friends was a young Jew called Kluger, whose father was chairman of the Jewish community in Wadowice. Lolek visited his friend's home nearly every day, and this friendship continued after the war, as did all the others. (One of Pope John Paul II's first private audiences was for Kluger and his family.) Until October 1978 the twenty-two surviving colleagues from the grammar school met every two years at the Archbishop's Palace in Krakow for a reunion. Cardinal Wojtyla always welcomed them enthusiastically and warm-heartedly, and was always 'just as we knew him at school'.

Lolek enjoyed meeting people and talking to them. At school he often took part in Saturday folk nights at the local park, where young people got together round a bonfire, singing and listening to poetry. Wojtyla himself had begun to write poems, and just before his matriculation he won second prize reciting poems at a Speech Festival organized by a well-known Polish actress. He was very keen on the theatre and was one of the first to join a dramatic society jointly organized by his own school and the private grammar school for girls in Wadowice. Here he took on the work of actor and co-producer, and excelled in the leading roles he played, many of them alongside the daughter of his school's headmaster. He is even credited with once having played two roles simultaneously – doing a quick-change act and improvising his lines after one of the other performers was taken ill. By all accounts his performance was superb. He is especially remembered in the title role of a drama by one of Poland's three leading 'prophetic poets' from the days of partition: Juliusz Slowacki, in which the main character wrestles with his conscience, God and a vision of the national destiny. At one time Wadowice's most prominent citizen was the writer Zegadlowicz, whose book had been banned by the Church because of its fascination with sex, but it was discussed in a circle of close friends with Lolek among them.

Lolek's interests ranged from academic to practically everything else. His friends still remember him as ruggedly handsome and athletic, popular with the girls (he had a steady girlfriend), with a prankish attitude towards authority. He was also an irrepressible raconteur. 'You couldn't help but like him,' one of his old schoolmates recalls. 'He seemed to radiate good cheer and lively conversation – a bit of a gossip, a bit of Homer, and the odd Latin quotation thrown in from time to time.' His kindness is also remembered: 'He was walking down the street on a bitterly cold day,' recalls Mrs K, 'and he saw some poor chap without a coat. He took off his own coat and gave it to him.'

Wojtyla was an outdoor enthusiast and sportsman, whose great passion was soccer. A schoolmate remembers him as an excellent goalkeeper: 'Our matches used to drag on until sunset, or until we were ordered off the field by the army detachments who also came to practise there ...' Sometimes they played in the street outside Lolek's home and got chased away and rebuked by the priest for kicking the ball against the church wall. They say that when the Skawa river flooded the neighbourhood, Lolek used to swim in the floodwater. He also took up skiing on a hill near Wadowice, and he loved skating, and going on long walks in the hills.

Two of Lolek's distant cousins who lived in Biala Krakowska remember him well. He and his father used to spend a day or two with them on their way to Biala Leszczyny, an hour's walk away, since there was no public transport available. They used to spend holidays, Christmas and Easter at Leszczyny with Lolek's aunt Stefania (his father's sister), who was a teacher in the local school. Sometimes she would come down to Wadowice instead to organize Christmas for them.

But whenever Lolek stayed with his two cousins and their parents in Biala Krakowska the two young girls were always afraid of him. He was older than they were, bright as quicksilver, bursting with energy and so full of life that he seemed to fill out the whole house with his personality. Yet for all that he was very well brought up, they recall, well-mannered and pleasant. Once one of the young girls who was left alone with Lolek in the house dived under the table as he grabbed a broom and a large potato from the kitchen and began to play hockey right there in the house. The potato bounced off the improvised hockey stick and hurled into the furniture as his terrified cousin looked on muttering: 'He's possessed! He's possessed!'

On another occasion Lolek and his father went to the cinema (he was a very keen cinema-goer) to see a Polish film. Afterwards Lolek did nothing else but sing the theme song from the film in his baritone voice: 'Barbara, you are the only one for me; Barbara, you are the only girl for me; all the boys just wink at you, because there's no one else like you ...' The following morning he leapt out of bed at dawn and ran to mass before breakfast.

The parish priest in Wadowice who had known Lolek since 1932 always hoped that young Wojtyla would finally choose the priest-hood. Ironically, a month before Wojtyla's matriculation the erst-while Archbishop Metropolitan of Krakow, Prince Sapieha, visited Wadowice and Lolek was chosen to welcome him to the school. 'He showed me a prepared text of the speech,' says Fr Z. 'I just glanced at it because I knew I could trust him. But I asked him to deliver the text from memory. He gave a very neat, dignified speech. Lolek's Polish was fluent and beautiful to listen to. The archbishop was very impressed. He turned to me and, looking at Lolek, asked: "Do you think we could ever make a priest of him?" "I don't know," I re-plied, "he's in love with the theatre and they've talked him into taking Polish philology." "A very great pity," said Sapieha, "we need someone like him."'

Yet somehow the young Wojtyla, the perfect pupil, the warm-hearted and faithful friend and colleague, was different from other boys. His teacher recalls: 'He stood out from others for his great composure, ability and versatility.' But there was also something serious about young Wojtyla. An extrovert? Yes – but he always retained a contemplative side, thoughtful and mysterious.

He passed his matriculation exams with distinction in 1938. Soon afterwards he and his father moved from Wadowice to Debniki Kra-kowskie, a picturesque district of Krakow, just across the bridge on the Vistula, built before the war mostly by Italian workers. He never lost contact with his friends and his birthplace, and corre-sponded frequently with the people he had known. Later as a priest and then as a Church dignitary he unfailingly came back to Wadowice to celebrate mass or other church ceremonies.

Whenever he said mass in Wadowice church, he would always point during his sermon to the place in the congregation where he used to stand beside his father and say: 'Here I remember my honourable father; here we two stood together before the altar of the Sacred Heart.' He always found time to have tea in the homes of his old school friends. And they knew that they could always see him in Krakow and count on his help whenever they were in difficulties.

In 1967 Cardinal Wojtyla was invited to Wadowice to celebrate the hundredth anniversary of his grammar school. Many former students and guests were expected to attend, some from abroad. The cardinal was due to say mass at 8 am and to deliver a sermon. But these were the years of the millennium celebrations of the Polish Church and State, and the then leader of the Polish Communist Party, Gomulka, tried everything in his power to downgrade the Church's celebrations. The conflict with the Church was then at its highest and the authorities refused to grant permission for the Wadowice school's planned anniversary only because the cardinal's presence could have turned this into an occasion of truly national proportions – something unwanted by the Party. But Cardinal Wojtyla arrived nevertheless, said mass as planned, and delivered his sermon. Then he toured the town and its park. At lunchtime the caretakers opened the gates of the school for him and he walked around the empty classrooms, looking back on the days of his youth.

Growing Up In 1938 Karol Wojtyla and his father moved away from Wadowice to Debniki Krakowskie. In Wadowice at least they had enjoyed their flat by the church with its proximity to schools and its large windows. But the basement flat at 10 Tyniecka Street which was to be their home in Debniki was a sad place indeed: hardly any daylight filtered through its narrow windows, the rooms were small and cramped, while the lack of sunshine made the place cold and inhospitable. Locals referred to it as the Debniki 'catacomb'.

With the summer holidays before him, Karol joined in the community work that most Polish students undertook during their vacations. For six weeks he helped out on a road-building site heaving building materials and carting wheelbarrows. Although he could not know it then, the day was not far off when he would be doing much the same work not as a community chore but as a matter of survival.

In the meantime the summer of 1938 slipped slowly into the pages of history, carrying with it all its notable events. It was after all to be 'peace in our time'. The young men of Europe breathed easily once more. The new term would soon begin. Life would be back to normal. With the start of the new academic year, Karol Wojtyla enrolled at the Philosophy Department of Krakow's Jagellonian University to read for a degree in Polish Philology. The department boasted a formidable collection of internationally known scholars and intellectuals: Pigon, Nitsch, Kolaczkowski. Under their supervision Wojtyla and other undergraduates in his year began their university life of lectures, seminars, tutorials, essays written in the small hours of the night, coffees drunk over long and serious intellectual arguments, debates, parties, gaiety and exams.

Professor Urbanczyk of the Institute of Polish Language in the Polish Academy of Sciences in Krakow was an assistant to Professor Nitsch in 1938. He ran the seminars in contemporary Polish grammar, and his classes held a terror for the students surpassed only by those of Professor Nitsch himself. Urbanczyk's name was mentioned with bated breath. Woe betide the student who gave the wrong answer to Urbanczyk's questions round the seminar table, or who muttered or stammered in nervous incoherence while Urbanczyk and the others looked on. But when all else failed, Urbanczyk would turn to Wojtyla, his brightest, most hard-working and dependable student. Wojtyla would get it right when difficult questions needed answering. Yet even he had to admit, years later when he was already a cardinal, that the memory of Urbanczyk's seminars was not a comfortable one. While visiting Urbanczyk at his home one day, Cardinal Wojtyla paused on the staircase and wondered if the proximity of his former teacher would still evoke that old fear he and his friends had felt ...

Wojtyla soon found that university life had far more to offer than just lectures and seminars. He enrolled in optional elocution classes, and took part in recital evenings organized by the students and held in the many townships near Krakow. He also joined the Polish Language Society, an august body whose ranks saw relatively few undergraduates. But the Polish language and its cultural background was something Wojtyla has always taken very seriously.

Many of the people who were in the same seminar group as Wojtyla have become writers and scholars in their own right, some with a considerable following in Poland. One such writer is Juliusz Kydrynski. He and Wojtyla became instant friends, drawn together by poetry and literature. They wrote poems and held literary evenings at Kydrynski's apartment in Felicjanki Street in Krakow, and attended all the first nights of plays staged at Krakow's theatre.

There was no drama studio or active dramatic group in Krakow at this time. Then in 1938 some of the writers living in the city set up a 'Theatrical Fraternity'. Their idea was to attract young working people and students into a venture where they develop and take a practical interest in the theatre. Wojtyla and Kydrynski were both quick to join. Some of the meetings of the Fraternity were devoted to theoretical discussions. But soon a play was chosen, rehearsals followed, and a full production mounted. Their first play was a popular spectacle called *The Moonlight Bachelor*, which was put on in the courtyard of what is today the University's Collegium Maius. Wojtyla, Kydrynski and a girl from Wadowice who, like Wojtyla, had acted in the school dramatic group (they had often played opposite each other) played the main parts. Other activities followed. The students joined Wojtyla in a visit to his old home town of Wadowice, and organized a literary evening there in early October. Wojtyla himself was among four students who not only read out the works of established authors, but had the audacity to recite their own poems as well.

Thus, right from the start of his university life, Karol Wojtyla submerged himself in the work and intellectual pleasures of the academic life. And yet he was not like the other students. Friends who were with him in those days saw him as something of a loner. He never joined in with the others when they went out with girls; he never went dancing. Though far from being an introvert – indeed all his dramatic successes seem to suggest an extrovert character – nevertheless there was a quiet, mysterious and meditative side to this lively, sociable student who prayed regularly in church.

He became friends not only with Kydrynski and his family but also with the Szkocki family in Krakow and their married daughter Pozniakowa. It was Kydrynski who first introduced Wojtyla into the household as his best friend. Thereafter the young man would come there regularly. For at the Szkockis' he could discuss Polish romantic literature with Madame Szkocki, and listen to works by Bach, Chopin and Beethoven, his favourite composers, which her daughter Pozniakowa played on the piano and which he could discuss with Mr Szkocki, a notable musicologist. He could even learn French at Pozniakowa's, for their lodger was a teacher under whom he studied the language hard throughout that year.

The approaching end of the academic year brought the summer

exams in 1939. Wojtyla passed in all his subjects, including the hardest paper of all: Professor Nitsch's descriptive drama paper.

With the students going down for the summer, another duty now awaited them: the Academic Legion. Here students were compulsorily put through the basics of military training while spending their summer at the Academic Legion camps. The drill and training lasted until the middle of August 1939. Wojtyla and his fellow students went back to their homes to enjoy a few weeks of peace and quiet before the start of the next academic year. In the event peace had but a fortnight left to run.

'There was no one left to serve at the altar for mass that day,' the former vicar of Wawel Cathedral recalls. 'They had all taken to the bomb shelters ...'

At the start of their Blitzkrieg offensive against Poland on 1 September 1939, the Germans bombed the main cities and towns. This was not what the world came to call 'strategic bombing'. It was the tactical variety designed to hamper Polish military effectiveness by sowing terror and destruction behind the front. As one of the major cities in south-western Poland, Krakow too was bombed on that first morning of the war.

Coming into the calm of the cathedral that Friday morning from the explosions and rubble outside (he always went to confession on the first Friday of the month), Wojtyla found he was the only one to serve at the altar, for war or no war, the vicar was determined to say mass. So, with Wojtyla helping at the altar in a cathedral deserted save for one or two frightened souls, and with the sound of bombs hitting the city outside, and sirens wailing from the rooftops, one of the first masses of the Second World War was celebrated.

Within a few days of war breaking out, the German 14th Army under List reached Krakow. The new military government closed down the Jagellonian University; henceforth the Poles would be taught craft skills only. There followed on 6 November a so-called 'Sonderaktion' carried out by the camp followers of the Wehrmacht, the Gestapo. The majority of Krakow's professors and academic staff were arrested and sent to Sachsenhausen concentration camp. Some were released three months later after interrogation. The majority never came back. The event is commemorated by a portal in the University's Collegium Maius which bears witness to the fact that the university never stopped functioning even during the worst periods of Poland's history.

You cannot deny learning to a people by military decree, nor by closing down its institutions and schools. By late 1939 those few academics who had avoided arrest, together with a growing number of students, had begun organizing themselves into conspiratorial cells. But these were not conspiracies to kill Germans or to sabotage their installations. They were underground networks designed to continue those selfsame university courses which had been closed by the Germans. Tutorial groups were assembled, classes held in the privacy of people's homes, examinations set and marked. The whole fabric of university organization and tuition sprang once more into being. Even makeshift laboratories were set up! Between 1942 and 1944 it was business as usual as far as all the university's pre-war faculties were concerned. And almost from the very beginning of the underground university, young Karol Wojtyla enrolled as a second-year Polish philology student in a secret cell under Professor Grabowski.

Wojtyla continued to live with his father throughout the early war years at their basement flat in Debniki. Two aunts (his late mother's sisters) lived above them, but for some reason little contact was maintained. Every morning Wojtyla continued to stop and pray at the local Salesian Fathers' church. His life-style altered in so far as the Nazi occupation of Poland had suddenly changed his status from student to unskilled worker, but Wojtyla's intellectual orientation was still in the direction of Polish language and literature. He continued his degree studies, as well as his various theatrical activities.

Wojtyla's most immediate problem however was to find a job. This was necessary simply in order to live and to support his father. But there was more than just a basic income at stake. To be unemployed in wartime Poland was to risk deportation to Germany as slave labour. Unless a man could produce an '*Arbeitskarte*' when stopped in the street, he could be whisked off there and then. An Arbeitskarte was thus a passport to holding on to such freedom as there was left to the people of Poland.

It was thanks to Kydrynski and to Szkocki's daughter Pozniakowa that Wojtyla was able to secure a job in a quarry at Zakrzowek, near Krakow, during the winter months of 1940. The quarry itself belonged to the Solway Chemical Works; the stones were needed as raw material. Kydrynski worked at the quarry as well, though the labour was far from easy and had little to distinguish it from slave or convict labour. The two men would set out across the Debniki bridge early in the morning. The cold was frequently so intense that they had to smear vaseline on their faces to prevent frostbite. Temperatures of thirty below zero Celsius were not uncommon. Wojtyla had come a long way from his easygoing student days. People remember him walking along shabbily dressed with a rucksack slung over his back as he made his way to the quarry. There he had to break rocks with a sledgehammer until he had filled a wheelbarrow which he would then have to push towards a railway wagon, empty, then return to break more rocks. And all this in the freezing cold. Perhaps he remembered the harsh lessons his father had taught him, keeping him in a cold room to strengthen his spirit and fortify his body.

Yet no matter how unpleasant the work, it is usually made more bearable in the company of friends. One such friend was to be found in the person of the quarry foreman, a Pole called Krauze. He was a kindly man, helpful and considerate. In time he 'promoted' Wojtyla by assigning him to the shot firer, another vivid and likeable old man. Wojtyla's new task was to pack explosives into the bore holes in the rock face and to string up the fuses. His new supervisor would come and inspect the work, shout for everyone to clear off, then light the fuses before galloping to safety himself. In his autobiographical novel *Tapima*, published after the war, Kydrynski wrote:

We envied Karol his promotion. It enabled him to spend the greater part of the day in a heated hut where he could chat with his 'boss' while awaiting another appropriate moment for blasting. It also detached him from the dull mass of quarry workers ... But apparently Karol was destined to distinguish himself from the crowd: not in vain was he appointed the archbishop of Krakow some twenty-three years later, and ultimately cardinal.

Wojtyla stood up to the hard work at first. As well as his daytime job in the quarry he spent his evenings studying in secret. But no matter how strong the human spirit may be, the human body has definite limits of endurance. Coming home from work one evening, Wojtyla collapsed in the street from exhaustion. As he fell, a passing German truck hit him. The driver did not bother to stop. Night came and he did not regain consciousness but lay in the street with a fractured skull until a woman found him the next morning and took him to hospital. She also advised his godmother of the accident, and told her which hospital Wojtyla was lying in, conscious now, though his head was covered in bandages. The godmother and her daughter frequently came to visit him in hospital.

In the winter of 1941–2, Karol was transferred from the quarry to the water purification department of the Solway factory in Borek Falecki near Krakow. His new job was to purify boiler water. He carried lime in buckets on a wooden yoke, prepared re-agents and mixed them with the water in proper proportions. The legs of his overalls were always white with lime. A daughter of one of the directors used to bring him rolls and cold meat to eat. One of his co-workers (today a professor of Krakow Mining Academy) remembers him saying often: you should live your life but not overdo your living. While working in Solway he became actively involved in efforts to improve working conditions in the factory and to provide for workers' religious and cultural needs as well as creating some recreational facilities for them.

Wojtyla continued writing poetry all this time. Some of his poems were published after the war in Krakow under the pen-name of Andrzej Jawien, in *Tygodnik Powszechny*, an independent Catholic weekly, and the monthly *Znak* run by Catholic intellectuals close to the Krakow Metropolitan Curia, and to Wojtyla himself. One of them, entitled 'The Quarry', expresses vividly and thoughtfully his experiences and meditations when he worked in the quarry.

> the stones know this violence.
> Yet can the current unbind their full strength?
> It is he who carries that strength in his hands:
> the worker.
>
> Hands are the heart's landscape. They split sometimes
> like ravines into which an undefined force rolls.
> The very same hands which man only opens
> when his palms have had their fill of toil.
> Now he sees: because of him alone others can walk in peace.
>
> Hands are a landscape. When they split, the pain of their sores
> surges free as a stream.
> But no thought of pain –
> no grandeur in pain alone.
> For his own grandeur he does not know how to name....

The young look for a road. All roads
drive straight at my heart....

There is silence again between heart, stone, and tree.
Whoever enters Him keeps his own self.
He who does not
has no full part in the business of this world
despite all appearances.

Wojtyla's spiritual and religious life was strongly influenced at that time by Jan Tyranowski, a tailor who lived in Debniki. He was a simple, uneducated man, very modest and ascetic. Inevitably there was a large gap between him and Wojtyla where background and language were concerned. Though he was an unimposing man with a crop of grey hair and childish eyes he had a truly charismatic character and enormous spiritual reserves. According to a priest who knew him, he was a complex and controversial personality. He would not bring himself to accept anything but the highest standards of spiritual life and expected the same from others – an expectation which was often above people's capabilities. Tyranowski drew his strength and dedication from the writings of St John of the Cross and Henri de Montfort. In his flat he would organize 'live rosary' circles of which Wojtyla was a faithful member. Tyranowski also formed the Catholic Youth Association of which Wojtyla was chairman. The Association would meet to discuss religious problems, and they would read the writings of St John of the Cross.

One of Wojtyla's first articles published by *Tygodnik Powszechny* and entitled 'The Apostle' outlined the personality and religious nature of Tyranowski. Later, as a cardinal, he referred to the simple tailor as 'an Apostle of God's greatness, an Apostle of God's love'.

On Sundays young Karol either went on long walks or played soccer on nearby playing fields. He spent an increasing number of his evenings with the Kydrynski and Pozniakowa families. Kydrynski remained in his Krakow apartment but the Germans had requisitioned Mrs Pozniakowa's flat (she had lived there with her two children; her husband was a prisoner-of-war). Karol immediately suggested that the family should move into his apartment in Debniki. In the event the 'catacomb' was too small for them, but they managed to find a house near Wojtyla's flat.

This soon became a second home for him. He treated Mrs

Pozniakowa and her children as if they were his own family. When he was discharged from hospital after the car accident, Wojtyla convalesced at Pozniakowa's home. Her mother gave up her bed for him and moved into the kitchen. While recovering there he avidly pursued his lessons in French. Sometimes he would bring Tyranowski back to Pozniakowa's, and together the whole family would read from St John of the Cross and from St Teresa. Workers from the Solway plant also called frequently to talk to Wojtyla, and they always made a point of calling on his name day.

After the outbreak of war the bonds of friendship between Wojtyla and Kydrynski were strengthened. Wojtyla and his father frequently came to stay at his home, where Kydrynski's mother (Wojtyla always called her 'mama') ran the household.

It was during this time that the two men began organizing Krakow's secret underground theatre. It all started with readings from Poland's romantic literature in Kydrynski's living room. Later these readings and subsequent rehearsals turned into clandestine theatre performances, frequently held at great risk. A performance for about thirty selected guests was given in Kydrynski's own flat just half an hour after a Gestapo search. On that particular occasion they put on a fragment of a well-known Polish play which Osterwa, one of Poland's most famous pre-war actors and directors, had performed in his theatre in Warsaw years earlier. And the great actor was present in the small audience that night; Kydrynski had met him by chance on the street and had introduced Wojtyla to him. Karol was fascinated by Osterwa, and the meeting made a deep impression on him. Later, Wojtyla and Kydrynski used to visit him frequently and talk about the theatre, or rather listen to Osterwa's monologues recalling times gone by.

Kydrynski and Karol continued to organize literary discussions at home and write poetry. They also ventured into wider literary fields. Wojtyla himself became a playwright. He tried his hand at writing plays on Biblical themes, for instance about Job. The extract below is on another theme – marriage. It was published after the war by the Krakow Catholic monthly, *Znak*, under the title: 'In front of a jeweller's – a monologue on the sacrament of matrimony interspersed with dramatic dialogue'.

ADAM: Love carries people away like an absolute, although it lacks absolute dimensions. But acting under an illusion, they do not try to connect that love with the Love which has such a dimension. They do not even feel the need, blinded not so much by the force of their emotion as by lack of humility. It is lack of humility towards what love must be in its true essence. The more aware they are of it, the smaller the danger. Otherwise there is the great danger that love will not stand the pressure of reality ...

Sometimes human existence seems too short for love. At other times it is, however, the other way round: human love seems too short in relation to existence, or rather too shallow. In any case, every person has at his or her disposal an existence and a love. The problem is: how to build a sensible structure out of it?

This structure, moreover, must never be inward-looking. It must be open in such a way that on the one hand it has to embrace other people, on the other it has to reflect the absolute Existence and Love in some way, at all times.

(translated by Boleslaw Taborski)

In 1940–1 Wojtyla was one of the first to join the new underground Rhapsody Theatre as an actor and co-producer. His lifelong passion for acting was finally being fulfilled. It was round about that time, according to some of his friends, that he formed a sentimental attachment to a young woman.

The Rhapsody Theatre was organized by Mieczyslaw Kotlarczyk, whom Wojtyla had first met in his school days in Wadowice, when Kotlarczyk used to help the school dramatic society. Kotlarczyk had had to get out of Wadowice (which was now in the Third Reich, thanks to Hitler's skill in cartography). He went to Krakow and at Wojtyla's suggestion moved into the 'catacomb' on Tyniecka Street with his wife. :

The conspiratorial theatrical group of three actresses and two actors (including Wojtyla) which Kotlarczyk gathered together initially called itself the 'Theatre of the Spoken Word'. The name summed up their activities. This small underground group was completely cut off from all normal means of dramatic production, all the complex resources of stage and scenery which characterize the conventional theatre. Only the living, spoken word was left to them, delivered by actors without fixed scenery behind them, in a single room with a piano or two as the only resources. As 'Andrzej Jawien' himself wrote after the war: 'The word is the key to dramatic ferment – a ferment through which flow the deeds of men and out of which words draw their dynamism.'

This discovery of the relationship between word and deed marked the departure point along the road to success for Kotlarczyk and his group. Between them they staged five premieres and twenty-two performances of plays by famous Polish poets and playwrights – all classics of Polish drama. All this theatrical activity took place in various private apartments all over Krakow before carefully selected audiences. Over a hundred underground rehearsals were held, mostly in the Debniki district near Wojtyla's home. After the war, Kotlarczyk wrote in his memoirs:

> Unforgettable Wednesdays and Saturdays despite terror and arrests. The rehearsals of works by the greatest Polish writers and poets went on, often in a dark, cold kitchen, sometimes with just a candle or two. But we firmly believed in our survival; we were sure we would reach the frontiers of freedom, always faithful to the idea of our theatre.

Wojtyla played main roles in many of the productions.

Some idea of the conditions under which the small group tried to keep the Polish theatre alive under the Nazi occupation can be gleaned from an eye-witness account of a poetry recital being given one evening by Wojtyla. He was reciting an extract from one of the poetical masterpieces of Polish literature, reading slowly, because these were the words of the dying priest Robak, in Mickiewicz's epic poem *Pan Tadeusz* (translated by Kenneth Mackenzie).

> ... I fought for Poland: where and how? That story
> I shall not tell: 'twas not for earthly glory
> That I so often faced the cannon's roar.
> I would remember not my deeds of war
> But quiet and useful acts, my sufferings
> Which no one ...

Suddenly a public address loudspeaker in the street cut in: 'Here is an announcement from the Military High Command! Our German forces have today defeated ...' Another triumph of Hitler's was blared through the streets of Krakow. Wojtyla did not stop; he did not even falter. He continued reading in the same quiet, determined voice, as if the harsh noise from out in the street were not there.

> ... The night was passing, over the milky sky
> The rosy beams of dawn began to fly,
> And, pouring through the windows on the bed
> Like diamond rays about the sick man's head ...

A masterpiece of poetry should not have to compete with shouted news of Nazi gains; Wojtyla did not try to raise his voice above the din. It just did not exist for him. The poignancy of the moment was felt by everyone in the audience as a surge of patriotism filled people's hearts. And it was all thanks to Wojtyla's refusal to let a reading from Mickiewicz be disturbed by more Nazi salt being rubbed into Polish wounds. Osterwa, who was present at this performance, sat fascinated by the actor's ability to express the triumph of poetry over the din of propaganda.

In one of his articles in the weekly *Tygodnik Powszechny*, Wojtyla, still writing as Andrzej Jawien, stressed the importance of this kind of theatre, in which speech plays such a dominant part and leaves relatively little room for the mechanics of acting:

It prevents the young actor from indulging in a pernicious individualism, for it forces strict discipline upon him. It seems that the most difficult thing in acting is to follow the character to be portrayed on stage. More often than not the actor remains himself, perhaps a different edition of himself, or merely in a different disguise. Kotlarczyk's theatre provided a general safeguard against this ever-present danger. Here there is no need for the actor to 'create' a character; his task is only to mediate, to present the given character to the audience. If this seems an easier task, it also demands a great deal of renunciation . . . The Rhapsody Theatre required a subordination of the actor to the dictates of the great poetic word. This becomes particularly evident when the word expands in faultlessly spoken choral scenes. A group of people unanimously, as it were, subjected to the poetic word has a sort of ethical significance: this solidarity and loyalty to the word.

There was another grimmer and less well-known side to young Wojtyla's activities during the Nazi occupation. Conspiratorial university classes and clandestine theatrical performances boosting national morale were dangerous enough in themselves. But Wojtyla also lived in daily danger of losing his life. He would move about the neighbouring towns taking Jewish families out of the ghettos and providing them with new identities and hiding places. He saved the lives of many Jewish families threatened with execution.

Dr Joseph L. Lichten, the representative in Rome of the Anti-Defamation League of B'nai Brith, has confirmed that Karol Wojtyla was active in an underground group collaborating with the Christian Democratic organization UNIA, which had a record of helping Jews. Because of this his name was placed on a Nazi blacklist. During the occupation he assisted Jews to find shelter and obtain false Aryan identification papers. After the war, when only about five-hundred Jews remained in Krakow out of a once flourishing Jewish community, Wojtyla helped organize the permanent care of the Krakow Jewish cemetery.

Karol Wojtyla and the father to whom he was so closely attached celebrated what was to be their last Christmas together in 1940 at Kydrynski's home. Soon afterwards the old Captain became seriously ill from a heart complaint and stayed at home in bed. Wojtyla would come to Kydrynski's house every day after work. Kydrynski's mother would cook meals which he would collect and carry home to warm them up for his father. One day in the early spring of 1941 he came to Kydrynski's as usual, after having first collected medicines for his father. This time Kydrynski's sister accompanied him to Debniki with the food. She went directly to the kitchen to warm up the food, while Karol went to his father's room. A moment later he ran out shaken and broken, and buried his head in her shoulder.

His father was dead. He had died of a stroke during his son's absence. With Kydrynski in the next room, Wojtyla spent the whole of that night kneeling beside the body of his father, and was lost for over twelve hours in prayer and anguish. Suddenly that mainstay of Wojtyla's life was gone. The man to whom he owed his existence, and who had been his frame of reference in morality, in religion and in life itself, was no more. It was a devastating personal tragedy. Now, at twenty, Wojtyla was practically alone in the world.

His father was buried in the Krakow military cemetery to which his mother's body was also transferred from Wadowice. The family grave is in the second row on the right-hand side of the cemetery. Wojtyla rarely smiled now. The blow had been so much more painful because he had not been present when his father died, just as he had not been at the deathbeds of either his mother or his elder brother.

At Kydrynski's invitation, Wojtyla lived in their Krakow flat for a number of months and spent many hours over his French each day. He eventually returned to his old home in Tyniecka Street to share the place with the Kotlarczyk family. And then, though he still continued to work at Solway's, Wojtyla suddenly enrolled at the underground theological seminary in Krakow.

Father Karol Wojtyla – Priest and Scholar   In following the thread of Wojtyla's life the sudden discontinuity in his decision to abandon philology and embrace the Cross is most perplexing. Karol Wojtyla is the only one who could disclose his innermost thoughts on this point. Yet for many of his close friends the move was neither as sudden nor as unexpected as it appears. That he was always deeply religious, though never pious, has already been shown by his regular church-going and his association with Tyranowski. The religious influence of his father was of course fundamental. Young Karol Wojtyla always found consolation and hope in prayers and meditation. The Church seemed at times to be a second home to him, though he was in love with the Polish language and its rich literature, and fond of the theatre, the cinema, serious discussion on all subjects, and various sports.

His friends – priests, school colleagues, acquaintances and even his co-workers – put forward three main reasons as finally determining his decision. The spiritual and religious influence of Jan Tyranowski was certainly one of these. Some suggest that he chose the priesthood as a vocation after having seen the appalling treatment of Jews at the quarry and at the Solway plant, where they were sent to work each day from a nearby camp at Plaszow; that he decided that the only way of saving mankind was to do everything in his power to achieve some kind of moral reconstruction. Yet the truth may be far more intimate. His closest friends suggest that the crucial moment came when he was kneeling beside the body of his dead father praying fervently for many hours, struggling within himself, analysing his life and his soul. Those twelve hours were for him a time of reckoning; a time spent wandering through an inner Garden of Gethsemane.

When it came, the turning-point was clear and unmistakable. According to Bishop Groblicki, Vicar General of Krakow, his first move was to try and join the Carmelite order, but he was told: '*Ad maiores res tu es*' – you are for greater things. So he sacrificed that great love of his life, the study of Polish language and literature, and enrolled instead at the Krakow clandestine Theological Seminary.

As we have seen, the whole of Krakow's educational establishment went underground in 1939, and all the former university's faculties continued their teaching activities. Theological instruction was no exception; indeed the contrary would have been surprising given the position of the Church in Poland's history as a national rallying point. But the problems were formidable. At a time when we in the contemporary world take education for granted, it becomes a chilling thought that the penalty meted out by the Gestapo to Krakow's hidden students was death by shooting or by internment at Auschwitz. Extraordinary lengths had to be gone to in order to protect students. Studies had of necessity to be on a part-time basis. Those who could be taken in as full-time students by the Krakow seminary were distributed among the various parish churches under various titles such as 'parish secretary'.

Wojtyla's studies at the underground seminary began in 1942 and were carried out for over two years on a part-time basis. He continued working at the Solway plant during the day. Life went on much as before.

Then on 6 August 1944, a few days after the outbreak of the Warsaw Uprising, Krakow experienced an event still referred to as Black Sunday. Gestapo and SS units descended on the city and began to round up all males found in the streets aged between fifteen and fifty. Shooting was heard in some parts of town. As word went round, so men began to hide wherever they could find shelter. No one knew whether houses were being searched. The occupants of Wojtyla's house in Tyniecka Street took no chances and scattered into hiding, but Wojtyla himself remained. He knelt alone in his cramped 'catacomb', and prayed. In the event the Germans did not search the houses.

But by now Wojtyla's days in his small flat were drawing to a close. The Archbishop Metropolitan of Krakow, Adam Sapieha, had decided that the war must surely be drawing to a close. It would be prudent to gather in his flock of seminarists scattered around Krakow, just in case there were more 'Black Sundays' organized by the retreating Germans. The theology students who, like Wojtyla, studied as part-timers were ordered to come to the archbishop's palace. There they were instructed to remove their civilian clothes and to put on the black cassock of the seminarist. The spacious drawing room in the palace was converted into a dormitory in which camp beds were provided for twenty students, including Wojtyla. Henceforth they were to remain in the palace, to study theology and prepare for the priesthood not as anxious men awaiting a knock on the door at dawn, but as fully robed seminary students close to their Church. Wojtyla had come in out of the cold.

A short time afterwards young Karol moved out of the drawing room and into a room selected for him by Archbishop Sapieha in one of the houses which formed part of the complex of the archbishop's palace; even the Germans did not dare enter its precincts. Sapieha, who had first seen Wojtyla as a schoolboy in Wadowice, had developed a special interest in the highly intelligent seminary student.

His time at the palace was not just spent in studying. The war and the occupation were still not over, and Wojtyla helped distribute newspapers printed by the anti-Nazi underground. His name was put on a list of 'unwanted persons', not least for his continuing assistance to Jewish families. Friends who knew him from the wartime seminary days described Wojtyla as friendly and physically tough, with a great talent for and grasp of philosophy, which he was fond of discussing at length.

But the move into the archbishop's palace, far from securing him a haven from the outside world, brought its own dangers. Of necessity Wojtyla stopped reporting for work at the Solway plant, and the personnel office reported the fact to the German *Arbeitsamt*. Warning letters began to pile up at Wojtyla's old flat at Debniki. Finally Sapieha himself tried to intercede with the Polish manager of the factory. The man was willing enough to help, but in fact his authority at Solway's was wholly nominal; Germans ran the whole plant. Nevertheless he was able somehow to arrange for Wojtyla's name to be 'lost' from the regular absentee returns forwarded to the Germans. The omnipresent spotlight of Nazi authority passed over him.

Wojtyla's certificates from the first two and a half years of his studies at the clandestine seminar (the 'Seminarium Clericorum Archidioces Cracoviensis') have been preserved at the Jagellonian University and in the Warsaw archives. They all attest to the excellence of his academic achievements. With the exception of psychology, which is acknowledged as merely '*bene*' (good), his standard in twenty other subjects was recorded as either '*eminente*' (excellent), or '*valde bene*' (very good).

Early in 1945 the war in Poland ended – a war which had seen so profound a change in Wojtyla's life, as indeed in so many others. Though the fighting was over and the Germans gone, a new anxiety began to grip Poland. Before the year was out, Wojtyla was nearly arrested by the Russians (who, of course, had 'liberated' Krakow) for joining in the singing of patriotic songs with a group of young people in a church square. Moreover, Poland as a nation was in chaos. The years of occupation and then the months of fighting by two gigantic armies had left the country looking like a smashed graveyard.

Krakow had at least been spared the worst; Warsaw was a sea of ruins and rubble. Nevertheless even in Krakow the damage had to be repaired. One of the first tasks of the seminarists was to roll their sleeves up and help clear the rubble from the site of the old seminary destroyed in the war. Already by January 1946 one wing of the neo-Gothic nineteenth-century building was completely restored and the seminary students moved in.

With the war over, Wojtyla was free to join the Theology Department of the reopened Jagellonian University. He enrolled as a third-year student in what was called the 'reduced session', since it started in March 1945. His studies were completed in the academic sessions, 1944-5 and 1945-6. His professor Fr Rozycki assessed his overall performance as *'eminente'*, which in his practical experience was excellent-plus. Rozycki regarded Wojtyla as a student of undoubted ability who under his guidance began writing a seminar paper on the part played by faith in the writings of St John of the Cross.

According to the Jagellonian University archives, Wojtyla was employed between November 1945 and August 1946 as a junior assistant, leading seminars on detailed dogma and the history of dogma.

Wojtyla's younger colleagues from this immediate post-war period remember him as an exceptional individual and outstanding intellectual who had an uncanny aptitude for discussing matters of a very difficult philosophical and theological nature. He was ready to tackle even the most intellectually demanding problems. Moreover he was a man who, when faced with a problem, carried out an extensive analysis of it and reached a theoretical solution before attempting any practical steps. Even then he fully understood the precedence to be accorded to a man's individual position, intellect and choice over any external institution. It was small wonder that all his colleagues gathered around him and came to Wojtyla with their problems.

Wojtyla's homily, a part of his seminar paper, remains to this day an unrivalled example of how a work should be written and presented. It was delivered not in church but, as was the custom then, during a meal in the seminary refectory. In it Wojtyla discussed the truth of fundamental faith and showed this truth against the background of personal misfortune and evil existing in the world. Because of his experience with the theatre, Wojtyla had an exceptional relationship with the spoken word. On 8 December 1945, on the feast of Our Lady, he had to recite a papal document on the dogma of the Immaculate Conception which was written in a ceremonial and official style devoid of any poetic undertones. The document was read out magnificently from memory, and his delivery brought out the hidden depth of intellectual meaning in the words. Yet, at the same time, Wojtyla's style showed the restraint and occasionally the fiery emotion of a firm believer. In March 1946 he published anonymously his collection of poems *Song of the Hidden God* in a Carmelite convent paper *Glos Karmelu*.

Karol Wojtyla was ordained a priest on 1 November 1946 by the Metropolitan Archbishop of Krakow, Prince Adam Sapieha, at a private ceremony in the archbishop's private chapel.

Wojtyla celebrated his first mass as a priest on 2 November. This being All Souls Day he in fact celebrated three private masses – for the souls of his deceased parents and his dead brother – and he did so in the unusual setting of the Romanesque crypt of St Leonard at Wawel Castle, among the tombs of Poland's kings and heroes. The following day, a Sunday, he went back to Debniki to say another 'ordination' mass, this time for his friends and old colleagues in his 'family' church of the Salesian Fathers. Then there followed a celebration lunch at Pozniakowa's home together with other priests, his friends. Before leaving, Wojtyla handed her a picture of the Virgin Mary, writing on the reverse side: '*Fecit mihi magna* ... Krakow 1.XI.1946' – the date of his ordination. In later years he would add in his own hand the dates and titles of his further promotions as he rose to become bishop, archbishop and finally cardinal.

Archbishop Sapieha sent Father Karol Wojtyla to Rome in the autumn of 1946 after securing a residence for him at the Belgian College. In Rome, Wojtyla began his two years of study at the Pontifical University Angelicum (Pontificium Institutum Angelicum de Urbe), beautifully situated on one of the hills above the city, and administered by the Dominican Fathers.

This was Wojtyla's first trip abroad. It was also the first time he was seen, assessed and sometimes admired by foreign prelates and professors – some of them among the most eminent Vatican intellectuals of the day, such as the then dean of the Theology Department, the Irishman Fr Michael Brown, Cardinal Marius Aloysius Ciappi, the French Cardinal Paul Philippe, the Belgian Cardinal Furstenberg and the man then regarded as the best theologian in Rome, the Frenchman Garrigou Lagrange. Thus Father Wojtyla appeared for the first time on the multinational stage of the Universal Church.

Professors and colleagues who remember him from those days all agree that Father Wojtyla had a tremendous capacity for work, which he undertook with perseverance and patience and with an uncluttered mind which could reach the heart of any issue and coherently analyse even the most complex problems. He appeared to make a hobby of tackling difficult questions and situations, and when he participated in discussions his arguments were both explicit and clear. He had the rare ability to express even the most complicated concepts lucidly, and to bring clarity, simplicity and perception to the most profound problems. He loved truth, and did everything in his power to go to its heart.

Wojtyla had a great range of interests. His favourite reading was still St John of the Cross, though he devoured other books in various languages, and browsed through stacks of them at a time, studying and reading into the early hours of the morning. As a result he became the intellectual soul of a large circle of students, set the tone and resolved various catechetical and evangelical issues. As always he was an extremely cheerful person, very pleasant, forthright and humble. His colleagues looked upon him with something approaching admiration, but he behaved as if he were unaware of that.

Wojtyla frequently went for walks and long excursions with his friends. He also walked daily to the Angelicum with one of his closer Polish friends. On the way they talked all the time, exchanging opinions, observations, and plans, and discussing Church matters and the immediate affairs of their respective halls of residence. He showed a great facility for forging contacts and sealing friendships with fellow students, whatever their nationality.

Father Wojtyla continued to write poetry at Rome – he had certainly not forsaken his literary interests. Sometimes he even recited it to his colleagues, the way he used to before the war, but it was difficult to procure any written copies from him.

The fact that Wojtyla lived in the Belgian College proved most beneficial, not only because it gave him the opportunity to acquire an excellent command of French, but also because it was there that he met Fr Marcelle Eulembroeck, a Belgian priest who was the secretary of the Jeunesse Ouvrière Chrétienne, a post-war working-class youth organization which aimed to secure recognition and dignity for young workers, and in which Father Wojtyla showed much interest. Together with his colleagues, he travelled to Belgium and France, encouraging others to familiarize themselves with the problems faced by working-class youth. Whenever he came into contact with young working people he was able to find a common language with them and displayed an intimate knowledge of their problems. Had he himself not known the toil of the quarry when barely twenty? In addition, Wojtyla also acted in a pastoral capacity to Polish workers in Belgium and France.

All these varied activities were fully supported by Archbishop Sapieha, as we can see from a letter Wojtyla wrote to Pozniakowa in July 1946:

The last few weeks of the academic year have been exhausting. Thank God the exams are now past and the pressure is off ... I am writing from Paris where I have come via Marseilles and Lourdes. The Prince [Archbishop Sapieha] expects me to spend the whole vacation touring France, Belgium and possibly Holland and studying pastoral methods there and visiting Northern France and Flanders with its Gothic heritage ...

While working at the Angelicum, Wojtyla became fascinated by the philosophy of St Thomas Aquinas. In a letter addressed to Pozniakowa's mother and beginning 'Dear Grandma ...' he wrote to her on 21 January 1947:

His entire philosophy is so marvellously beautiful, so delightful, and, at the same time, so uncomplicated. It seems that depth of thought does not require a profusion of words. It is even possible that the fewer words there are the deeper the meaning ... But I still have far to travel before I hit upon my own philosophy. Deo Gratias ... Karol.

And on 25 February 1947 he again writes to Pozniakowa's family:

My dears ... please believe me that time flies by with tremendous speed. I honestly do not know how the last six months have shot by. My studies, my observations and meditations all work on me much as spurs must work on a horse. Thus each day is filled to the brim with activities. This also gives me the feeling that I am serving God to the best of my abilities and according to His Will ... Karol.

Wojtyla studied at Angelicum for two years, from 1946 to 1948. He became a 'licentiate' in 1947, and the certificate in the archives of the Angelicum shows that he was awarded fifty points out of fifty. The same result was obtained in an examination required before he could submit his doctorate thesis: 'On the doctrine of Faith according to St John of the Cross'. The work itself, entitled *'Doctrina de Fide apud S. Joannem de Cruce'* was assessed at nine points out of ten by two examining professors, one of them Fr Garrigou Lagrange. But when it came to the defence of this thesis, Wojtyla was awarded fifty points out of fifty once more. He was unable to publish the thesis in Rome. Part of it has appeared however in Latin, and part in Polish. He became Doctor of Divinity, *Magna cum Laude*, on 30 April 1948 at the 'Angelicum Institutum Pontificium Internationale – Facultates Theologiae, Iuris Canonici et Philosophiae'.

And so Father Wojtyla, DD, left Rome, a city which he greatly admired. Writing to Pozniakowa in January 1947 he says: 'To discover Rome is a chapter ... which cannot be expressed in a few mere sentences ... There are so many levels and so many aspects ... one constantly comes across fine details and discovers an even greater store of wealth within oneself ...'

When Wojtyla returned to Poland in 1948, during the Stalinist period, doctoral theses could not be printed, but his studies and work at Angelicum were accepted at the Jagellonian University Department of Theology by the examiners under Professor Fr Wladyslaw Wichr, and he was awarded the degree of Doctor of Divinity, this time by the Polish university, on 16 December 1948.

The year 1948, when Wojtyla returned to Poland, marked the beginning of the darkest era in the country's, as in Eastern Europe's, post-war history. Stalinist terror was at its highest, and in the once proud nations west of the Curzon line, frightened men praised all that was unpraiseworthy and applauded deeds best left untold. The Communist Party in Poland purged its own more moderate leaders, particularly those who, while convinced Communists, looked for a so-called 'Polish Road' to socialism, different from the imposed Soviet pattern. Innocent people were being arrested and persecuted on the slightest suspicion of being either hostile to socialism or 'foreign agents'. Any contacts abroad, even family correspondence or listening to foreign broadcasts in Polish, led to reprisals.

A few years later the Primate of Poland himself, Cardinal Wyszynski, was interned in a monastery. The powers that be had decided that the road to socialism did not, after all, lead to Rome. Wojtyla thus returned to a part of the world where the dawn knock on the door was still expected, where prisons were full and beatings many, where the secret policeman was still his brother's keeper, and where the Great Teacher was neither Christ nor Buddha but the megalomaniac son of a Georgian shoemaker through whom millions had died.

In the midst of this Dark Age, Father Wojtyla began exercising his pastoral ministry in the small village of Niegowic, some 200 kilometres from Krakow. He was appointed as a vicar there, and left his mark on Niegowic in a very special way: the local church has a plaque boasting how it was built by voluntary efforts initiated by Karol Wojtyla. According to the church chronicle, the parishioners were discussing in May 1949 how to mark the fiftieth anniversary of the ministry of the parish priest. There were various proposals, and someone suggested painting the boarding around the old church. Wojtyla had a different suggestion: why not build a new church?

They did.

At Christmas time, when a gathering of young people led by the vicar visited people's homes and sang carols, it was a custom for each family to give some money for the needs of the church. Father Wojtyla took what was offered, particularly from the richer parishioners, and would give the money to the poor. Once girls from the Catholic Youth Association sewed a feather quilt for him, since the vicar had no personal belongings at all. Wojtyla accepted it gratefully, then politely offered it to three of the girls whose mother had recently died.

Though the people in the village appreciated Wojtyla, they felt that he was too good and too clever to stay there for long. Usually the vicars would stay for three years before moving on. Alas, in Wojtyla's case he was gone in one.

But then he would always come back.

For Karol Wojtyla never forgets his friends nor people who have helped him in his lifetime. For example, one of the first things he did after returning from Rome was to go to his old friend the priest at Debniki, to say mass in his church. Afterwards he knelt in the presbytery for a long time in quiet thanksgiving. His friend was extremely impressed and surprised at such depth of feeling, rare even among priests. The mass is always a deeply emotional experience for Wojtyla.

In 1949, Wojtyla was transferred as vicar to the parish of St Florian, one of the most important in Krakow. His aunt Stefania (his late father's sister), from Biala Leszczyny, where before the war he had spent so many happy holidays with his father, used now to visit him regularly at St Florian's and helped him run his household. She had no children of her own and, although the old lady was very devoted to Wojtyla, she nevertheless held two things against him: firstly that his house was always open to everyone; secondly that he would hardly return from one film before rushing off to see another, and always in the company of students and young people. It just was not in keeping with the status and dignity of a priest, and his aunt would shake her head at it all. Moreover, being orderly by nature, she tried to keep his house tidy, since Wojtyla showed no great talent in that direction, although he always knew where everything – from bits of paper to heavy volumes – was located.

But Stefania once quarrelled with him, not over the household but over a point of religion. She fiercely maintained that there was just too much sham in the Catholic Church. Having said so she later repeated her views to her brother-in-law, who was himself a deeply religious man. The brother-in-law listened thoughtfully, and without any hesitation replied that there could never be too much glitter nor too much glory where the Church was concerned. Finding no moral support in that quarter, Stefania resignedly reported his remarks to Wojtyla, who gently replied: 'I couldn't agree with him more ...'

Wojtyla's years of practice on the stage, his elocution lessons and not least his love for the spoken word all came into their own when he ascended the pulpit of his church. People who came to hear mass were very much impressed by what they heard and realized that here was a man of immense moral strength. Nevertheless, Wojtyla was criticized by some for letting his sermons go on too long. But most of the congregations found them compact and beautifully delivered, with the voice skilfully modulated to bring out the main theme of the sermon. Certain passages would be spoken with great passion. These observations were recorded by, among other people, an academic who is himself indifferent to religion but who heard Wojtyla preach at St Florian's. He attracted particularly large congregations to his sermons on the problems of Christian ethics, although the solutions he urged were far from acceptable to most people. He preached Christian asceticism and renunciation as a means towards spiritual growth and self-realization.

He certainly practised what he preached. Throughout his priesthood, and later as he rose through the Church, Wojtyla created the impression of having no concept of material wealth. This could be true, in that he did not attach much importance to things material. On his deathbed, Pope John XXIII announced that in his life he had sworn an oath to poverty. It is not known whether Wojtyla has ever taken such an oath, but he has undoubtedly acted as though he had. What is known is that as a young priest he used to practise self-affliction – quite by chance somebody once found Wojtyla sleeping on the hard floor. His indifference to matters of dress was complete; nor did he pay any attention to the quality of his sports equipment. He simply made the best use of what he had.

As a vicar, Wojtyla organized a group of acolytes from among the young people who attended the church. He was popular among his pupils. His methods of education and training were unorthodox, and were based on modern principles of teaching. He would often take his pupils onto a common near the outskirts of Krakow and there play football with them, wearing civilian clothes. All this was being done under Stalinism, when such work among the young by a Catholic required a lot of courage. (The Communist Party had its own youth organization, whose aims were somewhat different.) Many priests were being arrested for such activities.

But despite his new vocation, Wojtyla could never completely break with his love of the theatre. People working at the monthly Catholic paper *Znak* in Krakow recall a young priest in a torn cassock coming to the editorial office with the outline of a play on the Polish painter Brother Albert. Wojtyla's choice of subject is interesting. Brother Albert gave up his art in order to serve the poor, the disinherited and the despised. It was not a mere accident that this man fired Wojtyla's imagination, himself a writer in love with art. In one of his later works – before some power greater than his tore him away from his early artistic attempts and achievements – he took up another subject that was equally significant. He wrote on fatherhood. St Paul says that all fatherhood comes from God, embraces the whole of creation and is the source of fatherhood in the human family. In 1950 *Tygodnik Powszechny* published his poems for the first time.

Wojtyla pursued his pastoral duties at St Florian's from 1949 to 1951. Then, at the insistence of his former professor at the Theological Department of the Jagellonian University, Fr Rozycki, Wojtyla decided to undertake further academic studies. As a theme for study Rozycki suggested a thesis 'On the possibility of grounding Catholic ethics on the system of Max Scheler'. (Scheler was one of the founding fathers of modern phenomenology.) Rozycki approached the then archbishop of Krakow, Baziak, and obtained a dispensation from pastoral duties for Wojtyla together with a sabbatical for further studies, on condition that the young priest would take up residence with his professor at Kanonicza Street in Krakow. He was destined to stay there for six years, from 1952 to 1958.

Rozycki was able to follow Wojtyla's progress day by day during this period, and when the time came he helped Wojtyla present his work as a theological thesis. It was accepted by the examiners (Professors Fr Wichr, Swiezawski, and Ingarden) as a suitable dissertation for a junior professorship. (This process of so-called 'habilitation' – not common in British universities – is one whereby academic posts in some European universities are secured through the writing of a post-doctoral work deemed acceptable by the university.) The work was presented in 1953, assessed, and approved in the first half of 1954 just before the Theology Department was closed down by the Communist authorities. Wojtyla's was, in fact, the last 'habilitation' thesis written in the department. It was published six years later by Lublin Catholic University.

Father Wojtyla the priest was now soon to become Father Wojtyla the scholar. Already by October 1953 he was lecturing on social ethics at the Krakow Theological Seminary, and enjoying the university atmosphere in Krakow, where he himself had been a student. He developed an immediate rapport with the new generation of students he came into contact with. They used to call him 'the eternal teenager', for he relived his own student days when in the company of young people. But while Wojtyla was busy running his parish and organizing various activities for the Krakow students, his own powerful intellectual abilities had not gone unnoticed; interest in them spread beyond the immediate borders of the Krakow archdiocese. And it was in the ancient twelfth-century city of Lublin that interest was strongest.

Professor Wojtyla Lublin is a city unique in the whole of Eastern Europe. It has the only Catholic university functioning within that powerful Soviet magnetic field which tends to align everything towards Moscow and Marxism-Leninism. The university is wholly maintained by ecclesiastical donations and financial support from international Catholicism and the 'Polonia' – the diaspora of generations of Poles now living in the West. Its rector in 1953 was Professor Krapiec, and in that year Professor Stefan Swiezawski from Lublin first drew the rector's attention to the young priest in Krakow who, in spite of being fully occupied with his duties in the large urban parish of St Florian, had just managed to supplement his Doctorate with the next academic grade, the 'habilitation'.

After due consultation with the Dean of the Faculty of Philosophy, Wojtyla was asked to give a few lectures at the university. The following year (1954) these lectures became a regular feature, and just two years later Wojtyla was offered the chair of Ethics at Lublin. By the age of thirty-six Wojtyla had thus acquired the full status and dignity of a professor, and of the Head of the Institute of Ethics at Lublin.

But it was not an easy job. Professor Wojtyla did not give up his pastoral duties in Krakow. He continued organizing Catholic activities among Krakow's university students and also arranged retreats for them. The sermons Wojtyla delivered at these retreats were in fact fully-fledged lectures on Christian philosophy. Young people would come and listen in their multitudes. He now regularly commuted between Krakow and Lublin (some 340 kilometres) by overnight train. But no train journey is ever a substitute for the comforts of a bed, or at least the quiet of one's own room, and one of Wojtyla's colleagues recalls that however lively his interventions during long evenings in the 'conversatorium', it was often evident that the young professor was desperately fighting off the need to sleep.

The professorship did not cease when Wojtyla was made a bishop in 1958. A fellow lecturer and fellow commuter on the Lublin–Krakow express claims to have been the first to have suggested to his fellow ecclesiastics that they consider promoting Wojtyla to be a bishop. He had been impressed both by the young man's learning and his deeply felt devotion to prayer. Once, when the dawn was just breaking over the Polish landscape as the train swept along with its dozing passengers, Wojtyla's friend happened to stroll into the deserted corridor to stretch his legs and have a smoke. There, standing by the window and lost in the solitude of prayer, stood Wojtyla, rosary in hand. Many of Wojtyla's friends and colleagues have all been struck by his constant need to pray.

Yet for all the time spent in work and pastoral duties, the priestly philosopher somehow found the time to go for long treks in the Carpathians. Sometimes he would go with a group of students; at other times his hiking companions would be limited to one or two close friends. In fact it was on just such an occasion that Professor Swiezawski managed to persuade him to accept the regular professorship at Lublin.

On a similar occasion, this time at Fossa Nuova in Italy, where Swiezawski and Wojtyla were both attending the Thomistic Congress in 1974, the two men were out on a long and lonely walk after mass. Wojtyla, who was a cardinal by then, had just preached a superb sermon at the mass, which he had concelebrated with a number of other priests. The sermon so impressed Swiezawski that he remarked: 'You will become Pope, my friend.' Wojtyla looked at him for a long time but did not say a word. Four years later, in an exchange of letters from the Vatican, Swiezawski found that Pope John Paul II remembered the walk ...

But what sort of teacher did Wojtyla make in those early days at Lublin? What exactly did he teach, and what was his viewpoint on Christian philosophy?

A one-time student of philosophy at Lublin Catholic University recalls that the largest auditorium in the university (No. 33), where Professor Wojtyla lectured on Ethics, was usually filled to capacity, with students from other faculties lining the walls. The abstruse philosophical subject seemed to hold an unusual fascination for the young minds. It is not difficult to see why. Wojtyla's academic theorizing was thoroughly grounded in experience. Abstract principles were illustrated with concrete examples derived from the vast pastoral experience of the lecturer, and moral systems were related to real living men.

The broad theoretical framework of Wojtyla's ethics was Thomistic (based on the doctrines of St Thomas Aquinas), but unlike most

Thomists he stressed that the subject of any morality is the living individual. Personal existence is for him 'the supreme form of reality', and this reality has to be respected in its concreteness. The philosopher and theologian learns most from direct contact with people, and the priest's position is privileged in that he can draw from the most intimate form of interpersonal encounter, which is hearing individual confessions.

This 'personalism' was one way in which Wojtyla went beyond the Thomistic framework. The other relates to the phenomenological approach explored in his earlier thesis 'On the possibility of grounding Catholic ethics on the system of Max Scheler'. The attempt, by the way, proved abortive (according to Professor Swiezawski), and the result was a rather negative evaluation of Scheler's system, but this and subsequent encounters with the phenomenological school had one permanent positive effect. Wojtyla came to realize the importance of the concept of consciousness, particularly in ethical studies to begin with, but in the latter years of his academic career he increasingly stressed the need to supplement the Thomistic philosophy of being with an equally comprehensive philosophy of consciousness. In this way the phenomenological approach converges with the personalist approach. Thus to some extent he modernized Thomism and interpreted it in a way which could be understood by contemporary man.

Wojtyla used these modern philosophical trends in his search for a consistent conceptual framework for Christian ethics. For the substance he turned increasingly to the Fathers of the Church, and in 1969 helped to create at the university an interdepartmental research institute on 'Christian Antiquity'. This somewhat deceptive name means in practice an institute of patristic studies.

If man, and man in everyday ethical stiuations, plays such a big part in Wojtyla's Ethics, it seems appropriate to revert once more to those reminiscences of his academic colleagues which bear on the man himself. Never mind the fact that apparently he always had time and money for others, but never enough of either commodity for himself – that is supposed to be a commonplace feature of any saintly person. But in the case of Wojtyla his shortage of time resulted in his often being late for lectures. Students at Lublin used to say that their professor set his watch according to some peculiar Middle-Krakowian Time.

Punctuality improved when some of the seminars for senior

students came to be held in Krakow. But by then the professor was already archbishop, and this brought its own problems. Sessions were frequently interrupted by the untimely arrival of an official of the Metropolitan Curia on some urgent business. To make matters worse the Curia official would, to the acute embarrassment of Wojtyla, kneel down and kiss the episcopal ring. Wojtyla intensely disliked this long-accepted ritual and tried on this and several other occasions to discourage it by a gesture of the hand or something similar. On one particular occasion he found a radical remedy: to the amusement of the onlookers, he too knelt down before the priest. The remedy seemed to have the desired effect once and for all.

After he was made a cardinal, Wojtyla continued his association with the university of Lublin, and was frequently called on to assess doctoral and 'habilitation' theses. He is well remembered by his colleagues and students from those days in Lublin. Whenever he organized spiritual, religious retreats for the students it was not at the university nor in the church. He would take them sailing or climbing. They would walk together in the hills, each man meditating and thinking. Wojtyla would often walk by himself. Then they would sit together in the fields and talk, discuss or debate. He knew how to reach people's hearts with his words, and he was always listened to attentively and eagerly.

Wojtyla always considered himself to be no different from his students, and was accepted by them as such. Some of them referred to him as 'uncle'; he was popular indeed. At the same time he enjoyed tremendous authority among the students. He organized discussions with them in which he always showed respect for his opponents, because he felt that any conflicting viewpoint introduced new elements into a debate. He certainly argued his own case strongly, but above all he sought the truth. There were also discussions at professorial level between teaching colleagues at the university. One of these got so carried away into the night that the commissionaire, convinced that everyone had left, locked all the doors, and all of them, Wojtyla included, had to climb out through the window. Luckily they were on the first floor, but even so they were stopped by a policeman who took them for thieves.

There was a marked division in those days within the university's academic community between the clerical and lay staff. Wojtyla avoided the priests on the whole and spent his time with the laymen. Two of his best friends were lay professors, one of whom now lectures at the Jagellonian University. The very junior academic staff especially sought his company. Two of them, for instance, almost always shared a table with Wojtyla during meals in the refectory, which invariably consisted of a tasteless, watery soup. After he had finished eating Wojtyla would push back his chair, rock back and forth on the chair's two hind legs, and discuss whatever came to mind: philosophy, ethics, sport and especially theatre. Some of these younger staff were fascinated by his experience as an actor. Lublin was a provincial backwater in those days, and Wojtyla carried about him something of the aura of the outside world. He was a progressive priest, but in the best possible way: open and interesting to talk to.

One of the young assistants then, who is now rector of the College of Europe in Bruges, was always conscious, when talking with him, that Wojtyla was once an actor. His sermons too had something of the theatre about them in the way he would dramatize themes and modulate his voice. He took a certain delight in all this, though quite unconsciously, because it was all second nature to him and he was magnificent at it. Students and many of the lecturers were captured by his powers of oration. The young assistant who sought his company was struck by the depth of Wojtyla's intellect even then – an intellect which stepped far beyond the frameworks of Thomist philosophy and looked out over universal horizons not circumscribed by theology. According to his friend, Wojtyla was conscious of his talents and of his exceptional standing among the clergy. He showed himself to be very self-confident. What was not clear was whether this apparent self-confidence was real or whether it concealed an innate shyness.

Years later, when he was a cardinal, Wojtyla remembered this young assistant who had left Poland for the West in the Fifties. On a visit to a small village in the archdiocese where the young man's mother lived, Wojtyla called on her privately, saying: 'I knew your son in Lublin and remember him very well.'

The ordained staff at the university remembered him as an open, friendly man, with no stiffness or formality in his nature. He used to tell them, 'our task is not only to care for those who are already members of the Church but also for the whole world which is seeking God; we are called to bring Him to the world.'

Professor Wojtyla brought an intellectual atmosphere into all meetings at the university, but at the same time he was careful to maintain an air of simplicity and humility. He would often talk of the moral collapse of the West, a point which caused him much pain. His whole manner was one of almost ceaseless philosophical meditation coupled with a Christian, humanitarian friendliness towards everything which represents truth, beauty and goodness.

When Cardinal Wojtyla was elected Pope, the rector of Lublin University, Professor Fr Krapiec, boasted with justifiable pride that the Catholic University in Lublin is the only one in the world to have the Pope as its Professor of Ethics and as a head of department. Wojtyla did not resign his chair after succeeding to the Throne.

4
Bishop and Cardinal

On 4 July 1958, the Pope appointed Professor Father Karol Wojtyla, DD, as titular bishop of Ombi and bishop auxiliary at the Krakow archdiocese under the Apostolic Administrator Archbishop Baziak. At thirty-eight he was Poland's youngest bishop. Four years later, after the death of Archbishop Baziak, Wojtyla was elected Vicar Capitular, and thus for all practical purposes in charge of the archdiocese. On 30 December 1963, Paul VI appointed him archbishop of Krakow, and, as he wrote in his own hand on the back of the picture of the Virgin Mary given by him to Pozniakowa, he took over as Archbishop Metropolitan on 18 January 1964.

Just over three years later, on 29 May 1967, he was elevated to the cardinalate by the Pope, and became the second youngest living cardinal. After the Vatican ceremony where he was given his red hat, he wrote on Pozniakowa's picture: 'Cardinal 9.7.1967'.

Wawel Castle Cathedral in Krakow on 28 September 1958 was the place of Father Wojtyla's consecration as bishop. It was a very dark, dull day, overcast and wet. Inside the old cathedral it was almost completely dark, save for the flickering candles. With great ceremony Archbishop Baziak of Krakow placed the bishop's mitre on Wojtyla's head, and he, in accordance with the ceremonial rite, held it aloft a moment, praying all the while. Suddenly – and thus are future legends born – bright rays of sunshine burst through the stained-glass windows and bathed the new bishop and his mitre in clear, warm light. It was a scene worthy of great religious painters. An eye-witness remembers saying to her brother: 'He'll become Pope one day.' During the ceremony itself the silence in the church was shattered by a shout from one of the Solway plant workers, where Wojtyla used to work during the war: 'Lolek, don't let anybody get you down!' This was received with sympathy by the congregation and by the new bishop himself.

Fifteen members of the Wojtyla family, most of them from the little village of Czaniec, were invited to the ceremony. Shortly after the consecration, on his way back to St Florian's church, Wojtyla paid a brief visit to his godmother in Krakow (she was very ill by then, and could not take part in her godson's joyful event) so that she might see him in full bishop's attire. The robes themselves were secured for his old friend by Kydrynski. The Kydrynski family had remained in constant correspondence over the years with a Jesuit priest in Chicago, who used to be a hospital chaplain and had emigrated to the United States well before the war. They wrote to him, naturally, about Karol's promotion. Some weeks later an enormous parcel arrived from Chicago, containing a complete set of magnificent bishop's robes. It was a gift from a Jesuit father to a bishop he had never met.

Each new step through life brings fresh expectations but also regrets at the past left behind. Thus Wojtyla, the brilliant new bishop, was faced with the unwelcome task of moving from the flat of his friend and former professor Fr Rozycki at Kanonicza Street to the bishop's official residence in the Metropolitan Curia at Franciszkanska Street. Rozycki's place was his home; he had lived there for over six years. Yet move he had to, not only because of his new, dignified status in the Church, but also because an empty apartment would have been requisitioned by the city housing department. Many of his friends afterwards visited him often in the new residence and heard him complain: 'I feel as if I'm locked in a cage here!'

On a lighter side, another incident is partly confirmed by Cardinal Wyszynski himself. Wojtyla was enthusiastic about canoeing. In fact he was on a canoeing trip when he was appointed bishop. The Primate's office tried for hours to get hold of Wojtyla and finally managed to get him to come to Warsaw.

'The Holy Father has nominated you to become a bishop,' Wyszynski told Wojtyla. 'Will you accept? You know the Holy Father does not like to be turned down.'

Wojtyla thought for a moment, then said: 'Yes. But that doesn't mean that I can't go back to canoeing, does it?'

It did not, and he was back on the lakes in a matter of hours.

While out camping, he always took along a portable altar for saying mass. He would fashion a cross by lashing two paddles together.

Father Pieronek used to act as Wojtyla's secretary whenever as archbishop he travelled to Rome. He accompanied Wojtyla when he went there to receive his cardinal's hat in 1967. The archbishop and his secretary travelled to Rome via Vienna on 23 June. Cardinal Wojtyla received his nomination on 26 June in the auditorium of the Palazzo Pio, and his red hat from the Pope on 28 June at 6 pm in the Hall Dei Paramenti just at the entrance to the Sistine Chapel.

Wojtyla was penniless. The cardinal's robes he wore had been presented to him by the Felicjanki Sisters' Convent in Krakow. The Sisters had somehow managed to procure the necessary money, mostly from abroad according to Fr Pieronek. After they arrived in Rome, Pieronek had to borrow 200 dollars for necessary expenses from his colleagues in the Polish College. The newly nominated cardinal wanted to be able to observe all the rituals of the ceremony, and prepared himself for it under the guidance of the representative of papal protocol. Pieronek and Wojtyla were already driving to the Sistine Chapel when Wojtyla noticed that he did not have any red socks to go with his cardinal's robes.

'I just haven't any,' he confessed, so the secretary stopped off at various shops along the way to try and buy a pair, but it seems that Rome had sold out of red socks that day. 'Let's go to the Santa Marta,' suggested Wojtyla, 'some cardinal lives there; perhaps the sisters are doing his laundry and will lend me a pair!'

So off they went, but the sisters at Santa Marta had already done the laundry and returned the red socks to the cardinal. There was nothing to be done. Wojtyla received his red hat wearing black socks. After the ceremony, full of good humour and smiling, he said to his secretary: 'It wasn't too bad actually. I watched all the other cardinals carefully and two others also wore black socks!'

Wojtyla's reign in Krakow began almost from the day he became bishop in 1958. He is a man who tries to avoid undue publicity and therefore, only a few people know even the everyday details of his life.

He lived very simply in the old episcopal palace in Krakow. To this day a cardinal's insignia – red hat and metropolitan cross – hang on the inner wall of one of the wings. A bit further on, his apartment overlooked the park encircling Krakow's old town. From the splendour of the palace hall you enter a cramped corridor and a staircase much in need of fresh paint. The door is painted dark oak. Wojtyla's quarters comprised a small entrance hall, a large study and a tiny bedroom. Here stands a simple desk with peeling varnish and some papers, a simple bed with a worn bedspread covering it, and a colourful pillow with some gay folk decorations. On the wall hang a Renaissance Madonna and a Polish winter landscape. On his bedside table lies a rosary, next to a thermos flask and a glass. On the floor and just under the bed are a pair of used black shoes. Everything was always in its proper place. The room is just as he left it to go to Rome in October 1978.

Karol Wojtyla usually got up at 5 or 6 am. He celebrated mass at 6 or 7 am and then had a frugal breakfast in the kitchen: some white cheese, scrambled eggs, or home-made egg noodles and milk. He never attached much importance either to food or to clothes. As a cardinal he had three black cassocks, including the one he wore at home, and four red cardinal's cassocks. He had three pairs of shoes. The impression prevailed that he deliberately refused himself those dishes which were his favourites. He always fasted on the eve of Our Lady's feast day and on the prescribed days. When someone once challenged him about this, he replied: 'If the bishop doesn't set an example by fasting, then who will?' He would frequently attend the church of the Franciscan Fathers, especially in the mornings after celebrating mass, and sit in the back, in the very last pew, and quietly pray by himself. On Fridays he would privately perform the Stations of the Cross there.

Wojtyla hated to waste time and was always very busy, though he never seemed to be in a hurry. His whole day was planned, literally, to the last minute. Sometimes he would lock himself in his chapel for long periods, or else would not actually lock himself in, but it would be understood that nobody should disturb him, except, of course, when the chapel was being used for some celebration.

On days when he did not go out, he read books (in many languages) in a special small reading room from 9 to 11 am. If he held a meeting, his housekeeper would bring in weak tea, so that he could refresh himself. He does not smoke, drinks a little wine occasionally, and likes beer. A friend said jokingly that: 'If the Italians knew about his taste in wines, they would never have agreed to have him as a Pope!'

Wojtyla had neither a radio nor television for his own use, because he felt they were both a waste of time. He only read, wrote and met people. His office was open every day from 11 am until 1 pm to anyone who wanted to come and see him. For he is a man who attends to people's needs, who watches over people and is prepared to listen to them, day or night.

When Kydrynski's mother was dying in a Krakow hospital, Kydrynski went to the Metropolitan Curia in the middle of the night, woke Wojtyla up and begged him to go to her in hospital. Bishop Wojtyla dressed immediately and was at her side within the hour. She died a short while later. He would always make a point of visiting the sick. If, as sometimes happened, those he wanted to visit were somewhere inaccessible by car, he would walk. People would be seen crying whenever one of his visits came to an end. Somehow he always managed to win them over. At Christmas he would visit workers, particularly at Solway. 'This is my real parish,' he used to say. He baptized their children, knew the workers' problems and was always trying to help them.

He was tireless, sometimes putting in as much as twenty hours a day, and had the disconcerting habit of reading or writing while carrying on a conversation – and then displaying total recall of what was said. He even worked while being driven in his car. The first car he used was a Chevrolet inherited from Archbishop Sapieha. Then he had an Opel, which he did not like because it was 'too ostentatious', and he finished up with a Russian Volga. He did not drive the car himself: 'I can't spare the time,' he used to say.

When driving in the city or outside, he always had a full briefcase beside him and read all the time on the way. He could read in the car day or night because he had a special reading lamp installed, and a special flip-up desk so that he could also write. Even when he happened to doze off for a quarter of an hour or so, he complained about the time he had wasted. Once the car had to be specially driven back to the electrician's to collect the lamp because the cardinal did not want to waste four hours on the road without reading. On another occasion, the car's electrical system developed a fault in the middle of a journey, and the driver begged the cardinal to switch off his reading lamp or else the battery would run down and they would be stranded. 'Let it burn as long as it can,' came the reply, and somehow they managed to get back to Krakow.

Wojtyla remained a keen sportsman all those twenty years of his reign in Krakow. Many times during the year he used to arrange so-called '*dniowki*' for himself – days off, which he would spend in the fresh air climbing, walking, or more often skiing. He would never enter a restaurant or a hostel to eat on these occasions. 'I'm out in the fresh air,' Wojtyla would say. 'Perhaps you could bring me something?' And this an obliging seminarist or student would do. When he tired himself physically, that was when he meditated and thought things out.

The cardinal was an avid skier both in Poland and in Italy. In Poland he would often set off on his winter skiing trips after midnight once he had celebrated mass on New Year's Eve. Usually he stayed at the Ursuline Convent in Zakopane, the winter resort in the Tatra mountains, skied from 11 in the morning to 4 in the afternoon, sometimes for as long as two hours at a time non-stop, and then spent the rest of the day working. His favourite ski runs were the Chocholowska and Kasprowy Wierch (the highest peak in the Tatras). He often climbed the ski slopes on foot. From the parking lot to the Chocholowska he had himself towed on skis behind a sleigh. Later he used the cable car to reach the Kasprowy Wierch.

A friend of Wojtyla's, who describes him as 'one of the dare-devil skiers in the Tatras', adds: 'He loved the thrill of it, the sheer danger.' Once, during a midwinter interview with the head of *The Times* office in Bonn, Wojtyla gazed out of the window of his residence and sighed: 'I wish I could be out there now, somewhere in the mountains racing down into a valley. It's an extraordinary sensation.' Once, when told that no Italian cardinals skied, Wojtyla remarked innocently: 'That's funny. In Poland forty per cent of all our cardinals are skiers.' Reminded that there were only two Polish cardinals, he smiled and quipped: 'In Poland, Wyszynski counts for sixty per cent.' Someone once asked Wojtyla, was it becoming for a cardinal to ski? His answer was: 'It is unbecoming for a cardinal to ski badly.'

A woman from New Hampshire in the United States remembers that she once broke her leg while skiing in Poland and was serenaded in the nearby hospital by a group of fellow skiers. Only later did she learn that the guitarist was Bishop Wojtyla. On retreats he often took his guitar along and sang late at night with fellow priests. On another occasion, he was skiing on Kasprowy Wierch near the Czechoslovak border and was stopped by a militia patrol. The rather slow-witted militiaman to whom Wojtyla showed his identity card did not recognize the cardinal because of the ski outfit, and growled: 'Do you realize, you moron, whose personal papers you have stolen? This trick will put you inside for a long time.' When Wojtyla tried to protest his identity the militia man shouted: 'A skiing cardinal? Do you think I'm nuts!' Minutes later the whole story was clarified, much to the embarrassment of the profusely apologetic militiaman.

When Wojtyla was appointed archbishop, he took his skis and canoe paddles with him to the palace. The old housekeeper there was nonplussed by these strange things, which she fondly imagined to be some new sort of episcopal crozier.

Wojtyla seldom went on holidays by himself – he preferred camping, either with a group of young people or with a few of his intellectual friends. On occasional short excursions he would go out in the company of his former students. A car would take him to the appointed rendezvous where he met his friends, and then everyone, their knapsacks slung on their backs, would set off on a long hike. Later Wojtyla's car would be waiting to meet him at the prearranged place and time.

Once he was on his own. As a cardinal, Wojtyla stayed at a rest home for priests in Zakopane in the Tatra mountains. On this occasion his immediate neighbour happened to be an elderly priest from some provincial parish who, not knowing the cardinal, took him for a simple young sports-loving priest, and often used him for small personal errands and services, such as fetching tea. Wojtyla performed all these little services without a murmur, and it was only some time later, by accident, that the elderly priest learned that his young neighbour was, in fact, a cardinal.

Until the very last days before going to Rome for the conclave he travelled regularly to Biala Leszczyny, where he used to go with his father before the war to visit his aunt Stefania (after the war he arranged for her to be looked after in a home at Rabka, the sub-Carpathian resort). He had many boyhood friends there. It was the place where many of his young days were spent – days of playing, singing, soccer and church-going. He always said mass there, and afterwards held long talks and discussions.

Wojtyla always remembers his friends, colleagues, students and the people who have helped him during his lifetime. He always found time to visit and help them in turn whenever required, even when he quickly progressed in his Church career and took on ever greater responsibilities and more onerous duties. There is hardly a parish he has not visited or a church ceremony he has not attended. To this day a parish priest in Bronowice in the suburbs of Krakow remembers when Bishop Wojtyla consecrated his new church, illegally rebuilt from an old mansion house (planning permission for a restoration of the building only had been given), and said: 'My goodness, it's large isn't it?' And then he brought some other bishops around to show them how churches could be built after all. Or another evening in the same parish when Wojtyla, already a cardinal, led a procession of the rosary outdoors at sunset among the surrounding trees.

In September he would always take part in the retreat at the church of the Cistercian Fathers in Krakow, because there would always be great crowds there, and this would give him the opportunity to enjoy direct contact with people, something he always sought. Many times in Krakow the cardinal would come to the Franciscan church or St Anne's to hear confession like an ordinary priest, particularly during the Easter retreat. He wanted to get to know people, to listen and to help them. Bishop Groblicki from Krakow writes:

Wojtyla would go to the Sanctuary of the Virgin Mary at Calvary; his father used to take him there when he was a young boy; he would make his way along the roads leading to Calvary as a humble pilgrim countless times; he would come there as a bishop and lay all his troubles before the altar; he would unceasingly lead us to the Virgin Mary and sing her praises ...

Unless he was abroad, Wojtyla would never refuse to conduct a funeral service for old friends or for deceased family members of living friends. He also baptized their children. Once he was met at the airport, returning from Rome, by the daughter of his writer friend Golubiew, who told him that her second brother had just been killed in a car accident. Wojtyla drove straight from the airport to Golubiew's.

Wojtyla was very attached to his colleagues from the Polish Philology Department of the Jagellonian University where he had studied before the war, and usually attended their reunions. He was looking forward to their October 1978 reunion, which would have marked the forty years since he began his university studies, and he kept referring to that date, but then the second conclave was called and that was that. He hardly ever missed the Christmas celebrations organized by Krakow actors, and would share the Communion wafer with them and join in singing carols.

But frequently the cardinal would also visit his many friends in the evenings just for a chat or a discussion. He participated in the private meetings of a number of Krakow intellectuals, which though they were mostly scientists, were devoted not to science but to philosophical and ethical problems. For most of the evening on these occasions the cardinal would listen in silence, and speak only shortly before he had to leave. These short observations were often decisive, and tended to keep the scientists locked in further debate till the small hours.

But he also used to drop in merely for a meal and a chat, as when he would turn up for his favourite dish of Polish '*pierogi*' at the house of Turowicz, the editor of the weekly *Tygodnik Powszechny*. On one occasion Turowicz's four-year-old grandson, had to go to bed and was asked to say goodbye to the archbishop. He came up to Wojtyla, took both the latter's ears in his infant hands, pulled the archbishop down to his own modest level and made a sign of the cross on Wojtyla's face. The archbishop was in raptures. He maintained contact with most of his even distant relatives. For instance, he visited his godmother's daughter, an old retired teacher in Krakow, on her name day, bringing a layer cake with him. 'He has never forgotten a Christmas or an Easter,' she says. 'He either came to see me or, if he happened to be abroad, wrote a letter.'

Many stories are told by people who knew him of Wojtyla's remarkable memory for faces. As cardinal, he often walked round Krakow in a simple cassock. The present assistant at the Institute of the Polish Academy of Sciences, who used to meet Wojtyla many years ago as an altar boy, bumped into him unexpectedly on the street one day. He bowed his head in greeting. 'Good evening,' the cardinal replied, 'and how is your sister Mary getting on? Has she managed to get into medical school?' Wojtyla had remembered the man's sister, who years earlier had wanted to study medicine.

Yet always there was the lack of time; time to read everything he had to read, time to think, to discuss ... Once on a visit to Kydrynski and his sister, she jokingly asked him: 'Why are you in such a hurry, Karol? What work can you have that is so pressing?'

Wojtyla only smiled at her sincerely, but not without compassion. Later Kydrynski escorted him down to the waiting car. Wojtyla got in, instantly switched on his dim little light and began reading some papers.

Contacts with Young People   Since his early days as a priest, then later as professor in Krakow and Lublin, and finally as a Church leader in Krakow, Cardinal Wojtyla inspired confidence and affection among young people, and commanded their respect. He sought out and enjoyed the company of the young and took great interest in their affairs and problems. His support of social radicalism appealed to Polish students.

Despite an essentially traditionalist view of Church doctrine, Wojtyla has encouraged such modern departures as, for example, 'pop' religion. In 1975 he found himself in a church basement with three-hundred theatre-goers applauding a student production of *Jesus Christ Superstar*. Afterwards he spoke for twenty minutes on the importance of love and joy in the faith of the young. He went to their meetings and discussions, often sitting on the floor in the middle of a group of young people and talking.

A former Krakow student recalls such a meeting with Bishop Wojtyla:

We were fully conscious that we were speaking to, and found ourselves in the presence of, an exceptional personality. There was never any hint of formality or unnecessary distance in his manner. He answered every question put to him, and never made his replies too complex to understand, or dismissed questions as being too trivial. He treated as a distinct problem anything which perplexed or puzzled a person. Such problems required a specific attitude and answer. His answers were sometimes short, sometimes laced with good humour, but always sincere and straight to the point. Whenever he spoke his words struck a resonant chord in our minds, even though the problems he considered were not simple, nor did he offer simple solutions to them. His natural sincerity and personal charisma, as well as his exceptional ability to communicate with people, appealed both to our hearts and minds. His personality always acted as a magnet, drawing us to him.

Wojtyla sensed how some people found God through communal prayer while others found Him climbing high in the mountains or canoeing down a river. Discussion in which the most difficult problems were brought out by him in an exhaustive, accessible and comprehensive manner played a major role. He showed us the truth and taught us how to seek it. He steered our enthusiasm and idealism towards a proper goal, and had the ability to present questions about God in such a genuinely attractive light that our minds could not help but be deeply influenced by his words.

A girl student in Krakow remembers how Cardinal Wojtyla, following the old Polish custom, broke bread with a group of young people on Christmas Eve and everyone wished each other the best of the season. Her wish was that the Polish bishops should not be disappointed in Polish youth. The cardinal replied wishing that Polish youth should not be disappointed in Poland's bishops. 'You are my hope,' he often repeated to the young.

As another girl student put it: 'We knew that he was always there. We could always go to talk to him about our problems and ask him for his advice. He was always ready to answer.'

Wojtyla's pastoral guidance was not limited to university students alone. His care extended to the young workers. He understood the extent to which a running battle was being waged for the souls of working-class youth. He was only too well aware of the problems these young workers faced in their everyday lives: their living standards, their social problems, their work in the factories, their lives on the housing estates, the glamour and attraction of a wholly materialistic outlook on life and their wavering views on morality. He knew that the way to bring these young people to God was through a clear indication of the road they should follow, the dangers that surrounded them, and the need to strengthen their faith in times of trial.

From the first days following his appointment as bishop auxiliary and then as archbishop and finally cardinal, Wojtyla took a very personal interest in the Krakow Theological Seminary. He had lectured there until 1962 on social ethics and the principles of moral theology. His equal interest was in the work of the Pontifical Theological Institute which was set up after the Communist authorities had closed down the Theological Department of the Jagellonian University in 1954.

This deep interest in both institutions was not simply the supervision by a superior Church leader of a religious establishment. It was simple human concern and interest in the young seminarists themselves and their families. But apart from his pastoral attention he also realized the importance of a proper education and a correct approach to the problems of the modern world, both religious and socio-political, for the future of the Church in Poland. He treated the seminarists as his spiritual offspring, and knew all the students at the Seminary by name even before their ordination. Twice a year he would meet with each of them not as a superior but like a father. Having completed their studies, the seminarists from each particular year would organize a reunion, with Cardinal Wojtyla always present. He was with the students whenever they broke the bread on feast days, including Christmas Eve.

In this religious atmosphere the Seminary was like a single family. On Christmas Eve they would go together to the crib which was placed in the assembly hall. Then Wojtyla would sit with them by the Christmas tree – often on the floor – and they would sing carols together. In this way he made an impression on the seminarists and also indirectly contributed to the centring of religious instruction in each parish entirely upon the priesthood. The novices used to organize name-day receptions for him. He also came to the Seminary on St Nicholas' day, when they always put on a comedy show. St Nicholas would appear on the stage, turn to the bishop-cardinal and say: 'Greetings, fellow bishop!' and hand him a special present.

Wojtyla always took a full part in the life of the Seminary and shared in its joys and misfortunes. For example, in one particular family six people were poisoned by mushrooms and three of them died; the grandfather, the grandmother, and a young seminarist. The cardinal was in Rome at the time and called for prayers for the souls of the deceased. He also sent a telegram on the day of the funeral as a sign that he was spiritually and personally involved both in the life and death of these people.

When newly ordained priests were being sent to their first parish, where they would have to learn how to combine theory with practice, he would treat the new curate and the resident vicar as equals. 'You are both equally responsible for your parish,' he used to say. He also tried to ensure that young seminarists and priests travelled abroad as often as possible in order to become acquainted with the outside world.

Wojtyla's dealings with other people were characterized by a total directness. He would concern himself not only with the seminarists but also with their parents. One of these young men, who studied at the Seminary between 1965 and 1971 (and whose brother was also a priest), recalls how Wojtyla celebrated mass in his chapel and preached a beautiful sermon on the occasion of the young man's parents' fiftieth wedding anniversary. He turned to the small congregation and said: 'For the first time in my life I am celebrating the wedding anniversary of the parents of two priests!' Later he visited the couple at their home, saying: 'This time I've come to eat!'

Wojtyla would always remind his young seminarists of the role of the family. 'Your family is of key importance,' he once said. 'They are your first religious seminary.'

Seminarists and young priests alike were extremely attached to him. He never shouted anyone down; was never irritated; never harmed anyone. His solutions to particular problems were always accepted and acceptable, not just because of the respect he commanded but simply because his were usually the only sound proposals. He always subjected every problem to a thorough analysis. If a seminarist came to him with a snap solution he would say: 'Think it over, wait, make up your mind on this then come back tomorrow.'

The news of Wojtyla's election to the Throne of St Peter brought joy and pride to the young priests and seminary students at Krakow. But then the realization that he would never return brought its share of sadness. As one young priest put it: 'We've lost a father.'

Wojtyla would frequently arrange meetings with the younger priests. He counted on them and formed his own assessment of the younger in relation to the older priests – who did not always take this kindly. Perhaps he wanted to have a hand in rounding off their training himself. His main aim, however, was to 'incorporate' the young clerics in his plans for the future. He entrusted them with responsible positions both in his archdiocese and in Rome. He appreciated competence, and this was the major factor in his approach to personnel changes. If somebody was competent to perform a given duty then age did not count.

As a leader and manager, Wojtyla gave everyone great freedom to express their views, and listened with considerable interest to opinions which he did not share. He would not reject these in advance in an authoritarian manner, but would propose, as he put it, 'another way out'. There was an impressive element of dialogue in all this. His mind thinks in a number of dimensions, though this applies in lesser degree to economic or fiscal matters. Talking to him, one is aware of several elements which go to make up his attitude towards you: fatherly concern, intellect, godliness, mysticism and an awareness of practical matters. Any subject which may be raised, whether religious, philosophical or practical, is never looked at in isolation but in its total context.

Cardinal Wojtyla knows all the priests he has ever ordained by name, thanks, among other things, to the constant meetings which he arranged. As we have seen his memory is boundless and extends to the smallest details. For example, a second-year student at the Krakow Seminary came to the cardinal for a private meeting of the kind he held regularly with everyone in his charge. Wojtyla looked at the student, thought back for a moment, then began to recite a poem with which the student had welcomed him to his parish some years before.

His gestures and body language also have this multi-dimensional quality and, again, are completely natural. Once he was saying good-bye to five seminarists who were leaving for Rome. For each man he had a different parting gesture: he drew one towards him with his arm; another he kissed on the head; he clasped the head of a third and squeezed it with both hands. All this was quite unlike the pomp too often associated with a prince of the Church.

The education of seminarists in Poland was thus conducted under Wojtyla's powerful influence and loving care. The priests leaving Krakow had his example before them as well as his attitude towards people. It was not unusual for him to invite seminarists to his chapel for breakfast. There would already be a number of Church dignitaries such as bishops and archbishops at the table. Some would look askance at the presence of a raw novice. Then, after a better breakfast than could be had in the Seminary, a discussion would begin still in the presence of the novice.

'Anyone who looks closely and honestly at Wojtyla,' a former seminarist said, 'cannot say anything bad about him but must serve and defend him.'

And so, under Wojtyla's wing, a whole new generation of priests grew up: a legion of young, intelligent, modern and forward-looking churchmen. From their ranks will come the future leaders of the Church of Poland. These are people trained and ready to take up any responsible position anywhere in the world, and for that matter in the Vatican itself.

The only church in Poland dedicated to Wojtyla's patron saint, St Karol, is in Niepolomice, outside Krakow. There, in a beautiful Renaissance chapel, hangs a picture of the Saint. Cardinal Wojtyla used to go and pray there every year, if he could. There too he would receive name-day greetings. The idea was put forward by the parish priest at Niepolomice. From now on, although he is the Pope in Rome, services will be held there every year and each Monday crowds of people gather to say prayers for him.

Archbishop and Leader 'My Krakow Church,' Wojtyla would often say, speaking not only about his archdiocese but about the Church as a whole. He always thought about his own 'parish' within the context of the nation and of the universal Church, whose importance was to him paramount. Ecclesiology counts for a lot with him, and Wojtyla is fully aware both of the duties and responsibilities of the bishops, and of what could be called 'the fullness of priesthood'.

When he became bishop in Krakow and later archbishop, Wojtyla initially experienced serious difficulties with some members of the Metropolitan Curia. The Curia had traditionally considered itself to be both a privileged and an independent body, and was used to pursuing an independent policy. Wojtyla's position was difficult because, as a former worker during the war years, he lacked the proper 'contacts' and 'connections' or sufficient authority among the rather snobbish clergy, very many of whom were jealous of his career. Wojtyla once admitted before a group of close friends: 'Well, what can I do? When Cardinal Adam Sapieha [his predecessor], who was born a prince, looked down on them from his lofty height, they were afraid of him. But I simply can't impress them in the same way – not as a former worker.' Nevertheless, he soon established enough authority for himself through his own talents and personality. This authority became even greater after he was made a cardinal.

He managed the Metropolitan Curia very well in his own inimitably simple and direct way. The chancellor of the Metropolitan Curia lived with Wojtyla under the same roof. The two men used to meet every day, and eat at the same table, talking about the many aspects of the life of the archdiocese. Cardinal Wojtyla always listened very attentively, gently breaking the flow of conversation from time to time to elicit some additional detail. He would listen to everything being said, though it was evident that he was more concerned with obtaining a down-to-earth factual and detailed account of the matter in hand than someone else's assessment of it.

Wojtyla seemed to stand 'above' those he came into contact with as bishop and cardinal. There was undoubtedly a certain distance between himself and his immediate environment, although this was not a conscious, deliberately cultivated detachment. Nor was this the result of his high office – Wojtyla's ability to break down that sort of barrier is well known. He was in any case a gregarious, sociable man by nature, so that the last basis on which he would wish to establish or sustain contact with other people would be through his authority. What intimidated many people was his rich, profound and powerful spirituality, which was immediately noticeable, even when he was joking. His was a special kind of detachment, a detachment which did not estrange but drew one closer.

It would be difficult to call Wojtyla the 'ruler' of his diocese. He did not wish to 'rule' in any authoritarian, autocratic manner. He sought to lead – that is to say, to create the opportunity for people with initiative, people of independent mind, and possessed of a creative and healthy imagination, to work together. One has to bear in mind that Wojtyla's spell as archbishop of Krakow marked the start of a brave new style of government in that archdiocese. It was indeed a valuable experiment, the real importance of which will only be understood by future historians.

Wojtyla wholeheartedly embraced the decisions of the Second Vatican Council (1962–5) in which he himself actively participated when bishop and archbishop of Krakow, and whose task was to 'renew the Church', to adapt it structurally and functionally to the needs of the contemporary world. He insisted on the constant importance of the work and achievements of the Council, and felt under a powerful obligation to see to it that its recommendations be studiously put into effect, and that Polish Catholics should know all about the work of the Council and participate in the practical application of its teachings and decisions. The Council was a milestone in the two-thousand-year history of the Church, and indeed in the religious and cultural history of the world. But just as the Council's work is not contained merely in documents, nor have all its recommendations been put into effect, despite the developments which have taken place in the post-Council years. Wojtyla therefore considered his primary duty to be to promote and prudently encourage the execution of the Council's norms and directives.

Above all he favoured the development of a proper attitude towards the aims and achievements of the Council. One had to put into practice what had been explicitly stated by the Council, while whatever had been 'implicit' should be rendered explicit in the light both of experimentation and of emerging new circumstances. It was to Wojtyla's mind essential that the fertile seeds of teaching and deliberation which the fathers of the Second Vatican Council had

Karol Wojtyla with his mother

The house in Wadowice where he was born and the Church of Our Lady where he was baptized

Karol Wojtyla with his father in
Wadowice about 1928

At his first communion

The grammar school in Wadowice

Karol Wojtyla (in paper hat and shorts) in *The Moonlight Bachelor* when he was
a student of philology in 1938

With his godmother, Maria Wiadrowska, during the
late thirties

Father Karol Wojtyla
in 1948

The parish priest with his altar boys

Bishop Wojtyla on one of his excursions in the mountains, 1959

Visiting highlanders in the Tatra mountains

Cardinal Wojtyla receiving his red hat from Pope Paul VI in 1967

With Cardinal Wyszynski, Primate of Poland, (*centre*) and Cardinal Heenan,
Archbishop of Westminster, (*left*) during the 1969 Synod at the Vatican

LEFT Karol Wojtyla as a cardinal wearing the black cassock, which he preferred for everyday use

RIGHT Wawel Castle and its cathedral in Krakow

His study in the Archbishop's Palace

Skiing in Poland with Father Wojciech Cybulski

Visiting his friend Bishop Deskur in Rome on the evening of the election

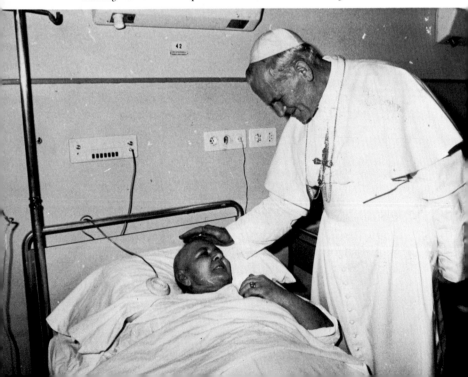

nourished by the word of God, and sowed in the good earth, should grow to maturity – a maturity of movement and life.

The bishops had to rethink their concepts of the nature and function of the Church, and its mode of being and of acting. This was not merely to develop still more perfectly that living communion in Christ of all who hope and believe in Him, but also to contribute towards a fuller and closer unity within the whole human race.

Wojtyla has a characteristically methodical approach to his work. Certain problems take a long time to mature in his mind, but once they do he pursues them with an iron though humane determination. His post-Vatican Council report provided abundant material for his later book *The Foundations of Renewal* (published in 1975). In it he thoroughly analysed the problems of the Church as a whole, and it was followed by practical applications of the Council's recommendations in his own archdiocese.

In 1971–2 Wojtyla initiated an Archdiocesan Synod, a unique experiment in the Polish Church involving the massive participation of both clergy and laity in its comprehensive work. It began with a Preparatory Commission formed by Wojtyla and for which he drew up the terms of reference. His ideas for the Synod were unique, and introduced three key elements: the study of Vatican Council documents; a spiritual retreat; and widespread consultation with as many people as possible both among clergy and laity. The aims of the Synod were to be an enrichment of the faith and encouragement for the laity. The statute worked out by the Commission was approved by the cardinal. He then formed the Synod's Main Commission and encouraged the formation of working teams throughout his archdiocese. Any such team would be admitted to the Synod provided that its mostly lay members were ready to undertake long-term work and were favourably assessed by their local parish priest.

Two problems arose: firstly, the fact that the teams had to spend between six and twelve months studying the work of the Vatican Council; secondly, the question of the number of teams to be formed. 'We could start with just fifty,' Wojtyla used to say. In fact over five hundred teams registered, and well over half of them got down to hard work. Their chairmen sat on the Main Commission. The teams attended the general sessions of the Synod together with officially selected priests and clergy. These sessions were intended both to disseminate information and to provide occasions for prayers. The sessions would hear reports on the various Synod activities, the future and current programme of work would be outlined, and then would follow a mass in Wawel Castle Cathedral, with a sermon delivered by Wojtyla.

The Main Commission's order of work when dealing with a topic would be as follows: a) examination of doctrinal principles; b) analysis of the present situation; c) recommendations. A paper would be prepared by the Main Commission for the various teams to work on. At Wojtyla's suggestion the first paper considered the development of faith within the family. In this, the third part did not contain recommendations as such, but a series of questions. Well over a hundred different lay-clerical teams undertook to consider the paper. On the basis of their many reports a second document was drafted which was once more referred to the teams at local meetings. New additional solutions were in turn proposed, which led to a third paper being drafted. This in its turn was sent back for amendments by the various teams. Finally the recommendations in their final form would be voted on in much the same way that voting took place at the Vatican Council: '*Placet*', '*Non Placet*' or '*Placet* – with amendments'.

Subsequent working papers were discussed along much the same lines, save that the third part contained specific recommendations instead of open questions. Voting was limited to those parties who had debated and worked on the particular issue. In keeping with the recommendations of the Vatican Council, voting by the Synod could not take place without a quorum which enjoyed a majority of representatives of the clergy. Thus the Church had to have a representation of at least fifty per cent plus one. Between 350 and 400 people would take part in the voting sessions.

The Synod as a more or less permanent body is due to be wound up on 8 May 1979, the 900th anniversary of the death of St Stanislaw, the bishop of Krakow murdered by the then Polish king. From the moment that he set down the guidelines and selected his people Wojtyla never interfered in their work, but if anyone had any misgivings or doubts then Wojtyla would go to that person or attend a session of the Main Comission to hear the problem. The cardinal limited his role to that of a consultant, or else to taking decisions which were either too difficult or risky for others to take; he never interfered or intervened in day-to-day matters.

There was tremendous pressure to put into immediate practice those recommendations which had already been agreed upon by the Synod. For instance, the recommendations of the first document have been sent out as pastoral material to all parishes. An enormous wealth of documents is emerging from the Commission, while the many people who have undertaken to carry out the work have themselves become both interested and involved in it.

In the course of the Synod various pastoral parish councils sprang up. The cardinal approved the basic statute of these councils, and sent out his encouragement for the idea, but there was never a hint of compulsion when it came to the formation of a council. The only condition was that the local lay team did their job properly and that the local priest had to obtain permission from the cardinal, which he would grant after consultation with the Synod's secretariat. The administrative and organizational structure of these pastoral parish councils provided a useful model for the whole framework of councils at higher levels such as deaconry and diocese.

As a Church leader, Wojtyla is very demanding on what he regards as fundamental matters, and he has always seen the need for total fidelity to the mission with which he has been entrusted. This he has expressed in the most absolute terms, with frequent references to the scriptural authority of his own office. He places much weight on what he has called 'the great discipline of the Church', which 'was not aimed only at multiplication, but also served as a guarantee of the correct ordering proper to the mystical body'.

The mystery of salvation which finds its centre in the Church and is actualized through the Church, the dynamism which animates the people of God through that same mystery, the special bond of collegiality which binds together the bishops, 'with Peter and under Peter' – all these are elements which require thorough reflection, in Wojtyla's view. The bishops must do so in order to decide, in the face of passing or permanent human needs, what the Church should adopt as its mode of presence and its course of action.

Love is the source which nourishes and the climate in which we grow. Fidelity means respect for liturgical norms issued by Church authorities. Faithfulness indicates respect for the great discipline of the Church. The fidelity of priesthood signifies viewing life from a supernatural perspective. For the faithful, faithfulness should be a natural responsibility of their being Christians. They should profess their faith with a prompt and loyal spirit, and witness it both by obedience to their sacred pastors and by collaborating in those initiatives and tasks to which they have been called. Wojtyla himself described the social role of the Church in an interview on Italian television in October 1978 as follows: 'We always try to be close to the people. We share their worries. This creates trust and it is the indispensable condition for fulfilling our duty and mission.'

As a Church leader he was extremely popular in Krakow and admired all over the country. He used to lead a quite irrational kind of life. As archbishop, for instance, he was for ever going to preach from one parish to the next, no matter how small they were. He put on weight and seemed to develop a slight stoop. But his health is robust and he is a very strong man physically. His sermons have become clearer and more precise according to one of his friends and admirers. Earlier he used to improvise his sermons and deliver them slowly, with long pauses during which you could hear his bishop's chain jingling in a silent church. Now he preaches very simply and fluently.

He never nursed a grudge against anyone, and has shown no taste for revenge, or even for one-upmanship. 'I was a witness,' his former professor Fr Rozycki tells us, 'to the occasion when, as vicar capitular, he gave the best parish at his disposal to a priest who had made vicious, personal attacks on him. In this he followed Christ's teachings: do good to those who persecute you. The campaign against Wojtyla organized by the priest in question became so serious that I considered it my duty to inform Bishop Wojtyla about it for his own good. If he had not taken the matter in hand, he would probably not have become archbishop, or cardinal, or Pope today.' Fr Rozycki did not disclose the allegations which were made by the priest.

Working with Cardinal Wyszynski Cardinal Wojtyla had a dual task which is quite unique: firstly in having to carry out his pastoral duties under a Communist regime, secondly in having to do so within the ranks of a national hierarchy which has for years been dominated by the personality of Cardinal Wyszynski, the Primate of Poland.

Although he was the second most important man in the Polish Church, even before he was elected deputy chairman of the Conference of the Polish Episcopate in October 1969, Wojtyla was at first overshadowed internationally by Wyszynski. At home, Wojtyla was regarded by the people (though not initially by the ruling Communist Party) as an equally resilient enemy of Communism, the more so since he was a powerful preacher, an intellectual with a reputation for defeating Marxists in dialogue, and a churchman enormously popular among younger Poles and workers. He was almost twenty years younger than Cardinal Wyszynski and he held the attitudes of a generation which came to authority in the Sixties rather than one still haunted by the appalling circumstances of the 1940s.

When Wojtyla was made cardinal in 1967, the move was widely interpreted by the Party as one which would counter-balance the so-called conservative influence of the Polish Primate both in the Church in Poland and in Church–State relations in general. Wojtyla with his intellectual background, his interest in poetry and literature and his doctorate in divinity was seen by the authorities as a progressive who would blunt the anti-Communism of Wyszynski. In the State-published encyclopedia there remains an entry containing the statement that at the Vatican Council Wojtyla 'represented a moderately reformist trend', while no such reference is made to Wyszynski. A subtle Communist campaign based on the well-known principle of divide and rule was fully supported by activists from the 'Pax' organization, a government-endorsed 'Catholic' movement which is Catholic in name only and was run under the leadership of Piasecki, who headed a near-fascist movement in Poland before the war. 'Pax' frequently cooperated with the Communist Party far more faithfully than the Communists themselves.

But it soon became clear that while the Primate was the Church leader who was willing to coexist with the Communists, it was Wojtyla whose attitude to human rights in Poland made him a target for official displeasure. In recent years the authorities have made it increasingly clear that they would not like to see Wojtyla at the head of the Polish Church, as Wyszynski's successor.

Inside the Church, however, the difference between the two men was never so pronounced. Such differences as existed were if anything derived from the respective roles they played. Wyszynski, as head of the Church, was concerned with the wider issues, while Wojtyla, who was closer to the problems of day-to-day life with the Communist authorities, was inclined to take a harder line in his statements. Yet there was a source of some potential differences in their divergent interpretations of the meaning and scope of the policy of '*aggiornamento*' (adapting the Church to the needs of the modern world), as well as of the reforms initiated through the Vatican Council by John XXIII and then continued by Paul VI. Wojtyla wholeheartedly embraced '*aggiornamento*' and soon became a spiritual example for the Catholic intellectuals grouped around the Catholic Intelligentsia Clubs, the independent Catholic periodicals and other publications of the Znak group in Krakow. Prompted by a desire to achieve a degree of political participation in public affairs, they looked at the Vatican Council reforms as a promise for an 'open solution' leading, within the Polish context, towards a potential accommodation between Church and State. They saw in Wojtyla, if not a spokesman, then at least a protector. But even here, when it came to a clash between the Primate and some of these intellectuals Wojtyla was an effective conciliator.

Cardinal Wyszynski, who was on the whole more concerned with existing political realities than with intellectual speculation, appeared by contrast to be a conservative and traditionalist, a man to whom the changes introduced by the Council might have signalled a threat to the cohesiveness of the Church in Poland; a Church with very special social and historical characteristics, in which simple but deep faith seemed to be inseparable from rite. Hence it was only natural that Wyszynski should have had his occasional differences with Wojtyla, who in addition had also transformed the conferences of the Polish Episcopate into a real forum for discussion, at which genuine collegiality reigned. Once any conference decision was taken, Cardinal Wojtyla would, after discussion, most faithfully implement it. His was the brain behind some of the Episcopate's pastoral letters, while he inspired others to be written and occasionally wrote them himself after they had been fully approved by the Episcopate. Human nature being what it is, even some bishops, envious of Wojtyla's intellectual stature and his successes at the Vatican, might have subconsciously contributed to creating the appearance of serious differences between the two cardinals.

Whatever their differences, Cardinal Wojtyla has always been uniquely loyal to the Primate. At one time the Party leadership tried to set up a rivalry between the two cardinals. Whenever prominent Europeans visited the country, officials would try to take them to Wojtyla first. But aware that he was being used, Wojtyla would either manage to be out at the time, or would merely act as an escort to Wyszynski's palace. When in 1967 General de Gaulle came on an official visit to Poland, he dropped his original intention of seeing the Polish Primate at the insistence of the Polish government. At de Gaulle's subsequent arrival in Krakow, Cardinal Wojtyla was 'otherwise engaged', and did not greet the French visitor at Wawel Cathedral. Instead, the custodian of the cathedral delivered a welcoming speech.

That same year, after clashes between Church and State over the millennium celebrations, the authorities rejected Cardinal Wyszynski's application for a passport, for the purpose of going to the Synod of Bishops in Rome, while causing Wojtyla no difficulties. He consequently refused to go himself, saying: 'We can only go to the Synod together, because . . . we constitute a delegation of the Polish Episcopate.' The then Party leader, Gomulka, continued stubbornly to oppose Wyszynski whatever the consequences, while the Church continued to show its solidarity with the Primate. It was at least the fourth opportunity for Wojtyla since he became cardinal to manifest his full loyalty to the Primate. Some time later, Wojtyla asked Pope Paul VI for his 'pardon' for the displeasure the Holy Father underwent 'not from our country and our nation, but, with regret we say, on account of our country and on account of our nation'.

When he received the news about his appointment as cardinal, Wojtyla interrupted a visit to a town in his archdiocese and rushed to Warsaw to report to Wyszynski and to receive his congratulations. On his return to Krakow, where he was welcomed by thousands of jubilant people showering him with flowers, the newly created cardinal paid his 'most reverent homage' to the Primate for whom, he said, he had brought 'a kiss from the Pope and that admiration which he enjoys in the whole of Christ's Church and all over the world for his unbreakable power of spirit'.

At the time of the Polish Episcopate's visit to West Germany in September 1978, and only weeks before the fateful conclave, Cardinal Wojtyla always took care to take second place to the Primate, and never hogged the limelight. He showed the greatest respect and deference towards Cardinal Wyszynski, and always stood to one side, as it were. It was important to him that the Primate was always seen as the leading churchman of Poland. The Primate himself described Wojtyla after his election to the Papacy in these words,

'When he has a mission to fulfil he does it with the simplicity of a son of the Polish nation who knows only one word to say to God: Yes!' On another occasion he said:

He is a man for whom prayer is a full-hearted manifestation of an almost childlike purity of faith. His rich philosopher-moralist personality radiates prayer at every moment of his being, regardless of whether he is performing his daily stations of the Cross or offering the most Holy Sacrifice at Communion, or whether he is carefully studying the children of God, talking to them, singing with them or showing them complex solutions to even more complicated problems.

Confronting Communism Wojtyla was steeled in the crucible of direct confrontation between the Church and the Communist-ruled State, but he retained the subtlety and flexibility of mind needed to cope with the great variety of less tangible challenges which face the Church throughout the world. He was a spiritual fortress withstanding the pressures of the Communist regime, and would never compromise on his principles. Yet he was able to place Church–State relations on the level of civilized dialogue between opponents, rather than of 'a cacophony of mutual anathema'. He was able to do this because he had the breadth of culture, the profound knowledge of Marxism (far better than that of most Communists), and the depth of intellect needed to challenge the Marxists on their own ground. The subtlety of his approach was to get the better of any argument without actually forcing the regime into a situation from which their only escape would be through the use of violence. The authorities feared Wojtyla for his wit, yet valued him for his statesmanship, at least for some of the time. Wotyla recognized the importance of giving expression to Polish national feeling – of which the Church is the most important embodiment – without allowing it to take an explosive form that would provoke a brutal reaction by forces from within and perhaps without the country. Nevertheless, there may be those in the Party to whom Henry II's fatal choice of words regarding Becket may have struck a sympathetic chord when faced with Wojtyla. If so, their prayers have apparently been answered.

While trying to avoid direct interference in temporal politics, Wojtyla has always implied an appreciation of positive temporal values and the need for interest in and help for human rights issues (sometimes by direct intervention, but mainly through the tool of conscience), thereby bringing a specific contribution to justice and peace on the international scene. His attitude has never been one of political quietism, nor of supine respect for temporal power. He says what he thinks, though he is careful to say it under circumstances in which he believes his words will have the most practical effect.

And what are these 'positive temporal values' Wojtyla has advocated? They are liberty, respect for life and for the dignity of Man, fairness in all dealings, professional conscientiousness at work, a loyal search for the common good, a spirit of reconciliation, and an openness towards spiritual values. All these he sees as fundamental requirements for a harmonious society, and for the progress of citizens and their civilization. The goals he has so often outlined also figure in the programmes of the government, but they have not always been achieved, and frequently not even attempted.

Wojtyla is, of course, uniquely equipped to conduct the far-reaching Catholic–Marxist dialogue. The circumstances of his surroundings have until recently required him to come to terms and coexist with Marxism, and in that he has done well. One is often left with the impression that he is more concerned about atheism than political Communism, since he realizes the challenge of atheism and agnosticism to the Christian faith and way of life. He was open to dialogue with the regime but he had no illusions and would agree to talk only on the basis of full reciprocity. There were no one-sided concessions. As a result he acquired a reputation in Poland for constructive discussion with the authorities, for having shown respect for the non-believing point of view. He has always discouraged the more militant forms of anti-Communism and the concept that the Church has the right to dictate to those who do not share its beliefs.

Wojtyla is tough but flexible, according to one Communist official. He is only too familiar with what separation of Church and State means in a Communist-ruled country – he has lived for years in just such circumstances, and is therefore an expert. But no matter what issues are being discussed with the authorities, Wojtyla will always maintain one condition: the safeguard of the rights of the Church and of the people. He also has a feeling for the realities of power in the Eastern Block, and knows what is and is not possible in Vatican–Soviet, and for that matter in Vatican–Warsaw, relations. Consequently he did not turn the flow of Church–State relations in Poland into an anti-Communist crusade, for this would have ignored those crude realities of modern Europe that the Poles understand so well.

Like Cardinal Wyszynski, so too Cardinal Wojtyla became a symbol of the Church's resilience, not only in Poland but also in the whole of Eastern Europe, as the alternative repository of a universal doctrine based on Christian rather than Marxist values.

Cardinal Wojtyla is identified in Poland as the chief advocate of still greater concessions by the State towards the Church and the people. The main issue is that of respect for all human rights, but in particular he has been concerned about education, access to the mass media, the elimination of censorship, the abandonment of atheistic propaganda and pressure, the building of churches, and freedom of religious instruction. He has been privately criticized by the government for his espousal of the concept that the Church must have a voice in social and economic measures undertaken by the authorities. This, of course, comes very close to being a political challenge to the regime. All the same, his greatest strength has been the ability to deal flexibly with the Communist authorities while defending and strengthening the position of the Church.

Thus Cardinal Wojtyla had over the years in Krakow gradually and steadfastly disappointed the expectations of the authorities that as a man with a reformist background he might break ranks with the Primate. The government may feel relieved to be rid of Cardinal Wojtyla, but it also seems to be apprehensive as to what policies the new Pontiff will adopt at the highest level of the Church's hierarchy.

When the government finally realized that the method of 'divide and rule' as applied to Wojtyla and Wyszynski led nowhere, the authorities began a programme of petty harassment. On at least two occasions Wojtyla was stopped and searched at the border on his way to Rome, and officials took away his diplomatic passport. Not accepting these indignities, the cardinal forced the officials to return his passport and respect his person. On another occasion, when he returned by train from a trip abroad customs officials confiscated his bags and returned them only after several weeks with a number of books missing.

But still the mild-mannered cardinal had his way. As at least one foreign correspondent in Warsaw observed, Wojtyla showed in major statements and sermons that he could be even more militant than the Primate when it came to castigating the Communists for setting petty limits on Church activities. In fact, according to former American ambassador Richard T. Davies, Wojtyla did not hesitate even to be confrontational when required, to the point of baiting the regime. From the time he was installed as archbishop in 1964, he refused to do business with low-ranking Communist officials. Once, when a local official managed to get through to Wojtyla on the telephone, he rang off saying: 'Until you officially recognize us, I don't see how we can talk to each other. Good day!'

Potocki, Wojtyla's friend and chairman of the Krakow Intelligentsia Club, recalls that the latter set a pattern of dealing with the authorities: action first and talk afterwards. It was surprising how little he gave away. He was tough and, at the same time, extremely adept at handling situations neatly. A case in point was the problem with the bronze monument for Archbishop Sapieha, which had rested for several years in the Metropolitan Curia. Wojtyla decided that it should be erected in Franciszkanska Street just opposite the Curia on a Saturday in May 1976. He gave orders explaining that no official permission would be necessary since it would stand on Church property. The statue was put up and ready to be unveiled. Then on the Sunday preceding the day of unveiling, Wojtyla's letter of invitation to the ceremony, which was due to be printed in *Tygodnik Powszechny*, was removed by the censors. Only then did the Curia write to the city authorities asking for permission. It was granted within four days.

Within the causes for which he fought and the official measures which he opposed on a national scale (the reader will find his assessments and reactions in a later chapter), there were three continuing 'local' conflicts with the authorities.

Wojtyla asked numerous times, and unsuccessfully, for the Corpus Christi procession to be allowed to proceed around four altars in the Old Market Square, as was the custom for centuries, instead of limiting it to the Wawel Castle courtyard. In one of his sermons he sarcastically remarked that even dog breeders were allowed to parade in the Old Market, but not the thousands of believers.

The second issue – still unresolved – concerned a campaign to restore the Theological Faculty at the Jagellonian University, which had been closed down by the authorities in 1954.

Finally, Wojtyla pressed very strongly to get permission to erect new churches, particularly in the large new housing estates. This, he said in a pastoral letter on 18 October 1977, was a test of the real respect for citizens' rights, of religious freedom and of the right of the Church to fulfil its mission as guaranteed by the country's Constitution. In that particular year only ten church building permits were granted in reply to a hundred applications.

Sometimes Wojtyla would intervene personally, and again in his own particular way. In the Nowa Huta suburb of Mistrzejowice, there used to be just a hut with some pews where catechism classes were held for local children. The authorities decided to demolish the hut. Then the cardinal himself suddenly turned up there one Christmas and said midnight mass. The hut was demolished – not by the authorities but by builders, to make way for a large and splendid church on the site.

A highlander's daughter, one of the parishioners in Kamasznica village, recalls how the village had been fighting hard to persuade the authorities to let them build a church. Enough money had been raised, but permission was still refused. So she led a delegation to Archbishop Wojtyla to seek his support. He saw them all. To quote the woman: 'I was most impressed. I thought I was speaking to a man who was already a saint. His personality affected everybody. You got the feeling that he loves you. He speaks to you like somebody who is a real friend, almost like a father.'

Wojtyla wrote to her many times afterwards advising her to pray fervently and to keep on working for the parishioners' wishes. His letters promised: 'You may be sure that everything will change for the better.' And it did. The church in Kamasznica is there today because Wojtyla and the parishioners kept pestering the authorities.

The Cultural Scene   As a Church leader in Krakow, Cardinal Wojtyla remained active in his scholarly, literary and journalistic work. It is impossible at this stage to list all his publications, or even to give an exact number of his various essays and articles. In Poland and in other countries various writers and journalists are currently working on it. The *Osservatore Romano* (12.11.1978) lists five published books, forty-four long philosophical essays and twenty-seven essays on theological-philosophical themes. On top of that over five hundred articles were printed in various Polish and foreign Catholic publications as well as some of the unknown number of his poems. The poems and literary essays appeared under the pen name Andrzej Jawien or simply A.J., which few readers identified as the archbishop of Krakow. He wrote poems all the time and the last one, 'Reflection on Death', was published in *Znak* in 1975, but under a different pen name, Andrzej Stanislaw Gruda.

His first book, entitled *Love and Responsibility*, was published in Poland in 1960 and subsequently translated into Italian, French and Spanish. The book was his own personal analysis of the problems of birth control, abortion, the sexual relations of married couples and other marital problems. Wojtyla's 'habilitation' thesis 'On the possibility of grounding Catholic Ethics on the system of Max Scheler' appeared in Polish only.

His other book *Man and Act* (published in Polish in 1969) summarizes Wojtyla's complex thoughts about the irreducible value of the individual. He finds a spiritual dimension in human interaction, and that leads him to a profoundly humanistic conception of society. The book deals with man and his right to freedom, the relationship between rulers and ruled, power-sharing, delegation of power and participation in decision-making. The text is difficult and highly philosophical. The translator, who lives in Krakow, asked Wojtyla whom he should consult as to the English text. 'Not me!' Wojtyla replied. 'My English isn't good enough.' Nevertheless, shortly afterwards they got together to discuss the English translation. Out of any two or three possible English words to be used in any context, Wojtyla would always select the most appropriate. He had his own queries on the text and fully understood the subtleties of the English language.

Wojtyla's *The Foundations of Renewal* (published in Poland 1975) provides his full assessment of the significance and impact of the Second Vatican Council. Finally his Lenten sermons given to Paul VI and the Vatican Curia in 1976 appeared as a book entitled *The Sign of Contradictions* both in Polish and in Italian in 1976. All these works are the fruit of a lifelong concern with vital problems concerning each individual and each community. They are presented in a language that is both understood and spoken by the younger generation.

Wojtyla's poems provide an interesting insight into his mind. They represent an effort to grasp in metaphor what still eludes a philosopher's analysis. One poem which appeared in a selection entitled *Pastors and Sources* (1963) seems especially revealing in this respect. Written in Rome during a solitary stroll through St Peter's Basilica, and probably under the fresh impact of the Second Vatican Council, it provides a glimpse of Wojtyla's personality, his links with the material world and his determined and hopeful search for the ultimate meaning in life, for integrity and oneness. To the degree that it suggests identification with the Rock of Peter, the poem sounds almost prophetic.

Marble Floor

Our feet meet the earth in this place;
there are so many walls, so many colonnades,
yet we are not lost. If we find
meaning and oneness,
it is the floor that guides us. It joins the spaces
of this great edifice, and joins
the spaces within us,
who walk aware of our weakness and defeat.
Peter, you are the floor, that others
may walk over you (not knowing
where they go). You guide their steps
so that spaces can be one in their eyes,
and from them thought is born.
You want to serve their feet that pass
as rock serves the hooves of sheep.
The rock is a gigantic temple floor,
the cross a pasture.

Wojtyla's preoccupation with the individual and his attachment to a spiritual interpretation of human interaction provided a foundation for his lifelong concern with the preservation of inalienable individual rights. Inevitably, this attitude led him to question the validity of the ideological basis of the Polish political system, and, as we have seen, brought him occasionally into direct conflict with the authorities.

His closest friends are the Krakow intellectuals of the Znak group, which publishes among other things the heavily censored weekly *Tygodnik Powszechny*. They are also closely linked with Catholic Intelligentsia Clubs not only in Krakow but also in Warsaw and other cities. 'He served his apprenticeship there,' says Bishop Groblicki of Krakow. 'The people there are his wards and spiritual children.' According to Jerzy Turowicz, the internationally known journalist and editor of *Tygodnik Powszechny*, and a friend of Wojtyla's, he began to work with the paper regularly in 1949, when he was already a vicar at St Florian's parish in Krakow. He had numerous long articles published, among them a cycle of essays entitled 'A Primer on Ethics'. His writings did not make for easy reading. His Polish was then rather heavy and involved.

When he became a bishop in 1958, and then an archbishop, Wojtyla's journalistic activities necessarily had to be curtailed. He would come less frequently to the *Tygodnik Powzechny* editorial offices, and although he still wrote contributions, they were no longer as regular as before. He used to send in his long articles in the form of letters to the editor. Direct contact between Wojtyla and Turowicz was rare after 1967; now that he was a cardinal, he simply did not have the time to spare. The weekly published some of his sermons and his pastoral letters – those, at any rate, which were passed by the censors. But he always maintained a lively and active interest in *Tygodnik Powszechny*, and in the monthly *Znak*, as well as the Catholic press in general. When the paper was in difficulties he would try to help by contacting the authorities, though indirectly. He would disclose the problems and difficulties at an Episcopal conference or else at sittings of the Episcopal General Council. The secretary of the Episcopate, Bishop Dabrowski, would then bring the matter to the attention of the Office of Religious Affairs or even higher.

Tygodnik Powszechny was never an organ of the Krakow Curia, but an independent weekly. Nonetheless there had always been informal links between the paper and the Curia since the days of Archbishop Sapieha. Wojtyla, as archbishop, introduced something different. He nominated Fr Bardecki, who was one of the editorial team, as his representative on the paper, and in that way the paper, and the priests working on it as journalists, were freed from the Church's *'imprimatur nihil obstat'* restriction. He was always their 'guardian' in more than one sense. In the Corpus Christi processions in 1977 and 1978 one of the themes of his sermons would be these Catholic papers, censorship and publication restrictions.

Wojtyla always had a friendly attitude towards the Krakow Catholic press, but sometimes a critical one too. He set up what might be called a private archiepiscopal press commission looking into matters touching the Catholic press. Turowicz and Fr Bardecki belonged to this commission, which met twice a year to discuss not just the weekly but more general matters too. This format, however, left a lot to be desired, and the cardinal changed it in 1976 so that the whole of the editorial board of the weekly paper and of the monthly *Znak* would meet him three to four times a year over dinner, held at seven o'clock at his residence. Afterwards they would discuss not only the problems of the papers, but also the situation of the Church in Krakow and in Poland as a whole.

Frequently the comments made at these meetings were very outspoken. He would sit there taking it all in with a smile, and then reply. The whole period of his association with *Tygodnik Powszechny* provided Wojtyla with a knowledge of matters which had hitherto been either quite foreign or little known to him, as well as an understanding of political problems. Their last working supper took place in June 1978. *Tygodnik Powszechny* has had articles relating to Jews and their problems. According to Dr Lichten, Rome representative of the Anti-Defamation League of B'nai Brith, 'there are very few Catholic newspapers outside the free world which would devote more space to the Holocaust, Jewish martyrdom, Catholic–Jewish relations. Cardinal Wojtyla played the guiding role in the operations of this very important Polish Catholic publication.'

Wojtyla was always a keen reader of *Tygodnik Powszechny* and of *Znak*. He did not read any other newspapers, except for those articles which Turowicz thought relevant and important and which he sent to Wojtyla. On the other hand he was an addict when it came to books. Before going on holiday he would ring the editor asking him to choose what he considered to be the ten best, most interesting and most important books – fiction, history, philosophy etc. – to read on vacation. He would take them away and return them afterwards, all duly read.

Wojtyla attached great importance to the work of the Catholic Intelligentsia Club (KIK) in Krakow and maintained very friendly relations with it, giving advice, help and his full support. His favourite choir, for instance, was the Academic Choir organized by the KIK, which he encouraged to tour abroad. He always promised them financial support, and they did not take him up on this too frequently, but once they did find themselves in a critical situation and needed 5000 zlotys (the average industrial wage is 4300 a month). Wojtyla began to rummage about in his pockets and pulled out 3000, then searched around in a wardrobe till he found the remaining 2000. He understood the value of the arts in the life of the Church, and the spiritual meaning of the choir, which sang hymns and took part in the Church's ceremony.

Twice a year he would share Holy Communion with KIK members. He also came to the KIK's twentieth anniversary in March 1978. After three lectures which he listened to carefully, Wojtyla celebrated mass in St Anne's church, delivered a most moving homily and then went down to the club for a chat with all the assembled members. His support for the real KIK was politically significant as well, since in 1976–8 the Communist Party tried to undermine these Catholic organizations by lending its support to a few fringe Catholic groups calling themselves Polish Catholic Intelligentsia Clubs, which were more amenable to some government policies.

Potocki, the chairman of the Krakow KIK, attended several meetings where Wojtyla was present and where, as Potocki says, he would always be involved in two things at once. They would have a meeting at 4 pm, then attend mass at 7, followed by supper and a discussion. In the middle of supper Wojtyla would apologize, leave the table and return with a pile of letters needing his signature. He would work his way through the letters with lightning speed, scanning the text of each one before signing it. Then he would leave once again and return with a pile of correspondence which had arrived that day. This he would quickly read, making notes in the margins. At 10 pm he would deliver a detailed summary of the discussions which had been going on all this time and make his own critical and creative contribution. When Potocki told him he had a multi-tracked mind, Wojtyla replied: 'You're right. Whenever I'm at a meeting and I can't be getting on with something else simultaneously, I get tired.'

One of Krakow's outstanding intellectuals, Jacek Wozniakowski, writes:

Our collaboration with Wojtyla was becoming even more profound. I mean that we gradually managed to shed those superficial, secondary aspects of any problem which can become so obstrusive, and obscure what is of real importance. With Cardinal Wojtyla one could be absolutely frank. Thanks to his extreme loyalty (a very rare virtue) and his confidence in others (what more demanding virtue?), our collaboration tended to expose its ever deeper layers and approach what is the real, though not always conscious, motivation of common endeavour and the real aim in our 'pilgrimage to the Kingdom of the Father'.

Wojtyla would try to help in many scholarly and literary activities. One of his friends writes about the cardinal's passion for research, his advocacy of Christian personalism, and the encouragement he gave to other researchers. While he was presiding over the Research Commission of the Polish Episcopate, Wojtyla was instrumental in the organization of the congresses of Polish theologians which take place every five years. Among the activities which enjoyed his support was the initiative of the Jagellonian University to reprint the oldest Polish Bible. Money was available from abroad for this venture, but at the time the authorities refused permission for publication.

In other fields, Wojtyla helped a great deal in the organization of the International Congress of Philosophers in Poland, and he travelled to Rome especially to chair one of the commissions of the International Thomist Congress. This international gathering of Thomists in 1974 was described by Josef Pieper of Münster as 'the Congress of the Cardinal from Krakow'. Wojtyla's lecture at this meeting: 'The Personal Structure of Self-Determination' was devoted to problems facing man in the contemporary world. The cardinal's many contributions to the debate electrified the participants who had gathered from all over the world. A popular saying made the rounds among those assembled: 'It is a real phenomenon for the cardinal to be a phenomenologist.' Wojtyla was unable to attend in person the International Phenomenological Colloquium organized by the Société International pour l'Etude Husserl et de la Phénomenologie in 1975 but he submitted his paper: 'Soi et Autrui – la Crise de l'irréductible dans l'homme'. It created a sensation. Later he lectured on the same subject at the University of Fribourg in Switzerland and also at Harvard.

Cardinal Wojtyla was deeply interested in phenomenology. His pastoral duties and his activities in Rome prevented him from attending other colloquia or congresses, but he never missed an opportunity to study or write on the subject. His two papers 'La subjectivité et l'irréductible dans l'homme' and 'The transcendence of the Person in Act and Man's Autoteleology' sent respectively to phenomenological colloquia and congresses in Paris 1975 and Arezzo-Siena 1976 were immediately printed in a worldwide phenomenological publication. He subsequently had a chance to lecture along similar lines at the Gregorianum University in Rome and opened the Philosophical Congress in Genoa in 1976. While he was cardinal, Wojtyla also worked on two new subjects: theology of the body and theology of justification. He remained a true, deeply involved and hard-working scholar till the very end of his reign in Krakow.

Wojtyla never forgot that he was the Head of the Chair of Ethics at the Philosophy Department of the Catholic University in Lublin. With the accumulation of heavy duties as bishop and later as arch-bishop he could only occasionally travel to Lublin to lecture person-ally. Advanced students had to come from Lublin to Krakow to attend doctorate seminars led and supervised by Professor Wojtyla. Initially they assembled at Kanonicza Street where he stayed for over six years with his former teacher Father Rozycki and then at the Archbishop's Palace. From three till midnight Wojtyla dis-cussed with his students their work and problems, always making sure that tea, coffee and finally dinner was served for them. The location of the meeting was changed when he was made cardinal and could not spare even these few hours. He did however find a solution. Essentially an outdoor man, Wojtyla needed fresh air and relaxation somewhere in the forests in a natural environment. So he would take his students to the hills and forests outside Krakow. There they sat down under the trees and discussed their doctoral theses. In September 1978 on one such outdoor occasion Wojtyla planned with the departmental academic staff the future of the In-stitute of Ethics at Lublin University. On 2 October 1978, the day before he left for the historic conclave, he sent by letter his last, very positive assessment of the doctoral thesis of one of his students. The letter was read on 20 November 1978, when the young man received the doctor's degree in Lublin, and his professor was by then far away in the Vatican as John Paul II.

Wojtyla also gave support to lay organizations like the Forum Laicatum, to which he attached great importance. It was of special personal concern to him that the most suitable Polish lay repre-sentatives should go to Rome and stand for the higher offices in the organization, and Wojtyla went to considerable trouble for this pur-pose. In an entirely different field, it was the cardinal's idea that the famous Polish nineteenth-century drama, *Forefather's Eve*, written by Mickiewicz, one of Poland's foremost poets, should be staged in the Dominican church in Krakow. (The play was also seen in London where it was staged in Southwark Cathedral as part of the International Theatre Festival.) In short, the cardinal tried to be everywhere and to do everything. He managed it all successfully, thanks to his constant passion for listening, participating and help-ing others.

5

The Vatican and Beyond

It is fascinating to observe how over the years the archibishop of Krakow grew in stature internationally; how a Church leader known throughout Poland slowly became a personality walking the world stage and especially at the centre of the universal Church at the Vatican. The very first obscure steps in this arena were of course taken when he studied at the Pontifical University Angelicum in Rome and journeyed to France and Belgium, but it was at the Second Vatican Council and then at the subsequent Synods of Bishops in Rome that Wojtyla made his name.

All the sessions of the Vatican Council (1962–5) saw him in attendance, first as a young bishop of forty-two, and then as archbishop. In all, the Polish Church leader made eight speeches, the most memorable being in favour of religious freedom. The Council opened his eyes to the greater issues of the Church in the world and its deliberations came to command his total loyalty. At the time he made some theologically conservative but open-minded interventions, some of them of great value. For Wojtyla, the Vatican Council was an event of immense importance, but he repeatedly stressed that the many documents coming from the Council were not dead sheets of paper but nuclei which should grow, be explored and lived in the life of the Church. They point the way to the Church's mission and its approach to ecumenism, its organic growth as well as its discipline. Even then he had no narrow conception of the Church – he saw it as the universal sacrament for all.

The contributions which Wojtyla made were marked by a consistent openness. During discussions on the Constitution of the Church Lumen Gentium – its internal organization – he urged that the Church must be primarily considered as the 'people of God', and only then should the position of the hierarchy be defined. The Lumen Gentium was the Magna Carta of the Church, as far as Wojtyla was concerned. He made considerable contributions to the editing of Scheme XII, 'The Church in the Modern World – *Gaudium et Spes*', and stressed the immense importance of the objectives set in the document and the need for the Council to work these out with utmost care. The document should recognize the multifarious and multinational character of the world. Advising a fundamental change of policy, Wojtyla spoke out against applying generalizations, and particularly those which smacked of moralizing. Arguments of natural law should be put forward.

The document affected the relationship between the Church and the outside world. Wojtyla suggested that the Church should present itself to that world, reveal its *raison d'être* and define its objective. If the Church wanted to reach people today, it must take up their real problems and defend their rights. He said:

It is not possible [for the Church] to speak at one and the same time to all men, to Catholics and non-Catholics, to believers and non-believers. It is not possible [for the Church] to address herself to those who are outside the Church, to those who attack her, to those who do not believe in God, in the same language as she speaks to the faithful. . . . It is necessary to underline even more strongly the significance of the salvation achieved by Christ on the Cross. A pastoral concern (for unbelievers) cannot prescind from the work of redemption which must be considered as a proper and constitutive element of the entire schema. The dialogue with the world cannot have as its aim simply the common good and the advancement of good principles, because the Church must not renounce its unique task, its mission of salvation. The Church undoubtedly contributes also to the temporal good of men but she places herself at their service so that, above all else, they can reach their true end, eternal salvation. . . . Let us avoid the spirit of monopolizing and moralizing. One of the major faults of 'Gaudium et Spes' is that in it the Church appears authoritarian.

Indeed from the tone of many of his subsequent speeches it was clear that he was against giving any impression of an authoritarian Church.

Another aspect of Wojtyla's personality was revealed in the Council, that of 'reconciler' – a role which has always characterized his pastorate in Poland. He firmly opposed the demands for an outright condemnation of atheism – it would be counterproductive. At the same time he equally firmly opposed efforts by some of the more conservative clergy to drop the declaration on religious liberty, which he and other East European bishops felt would be of assistance to them in their dealings with the Communist governments in their countries. The declaration on religious liberty, '*Dignitatis Humanae*', was eventually enacted and has become a crucial achievement of the Council.

As for atheism, Wojtyla argued that a human being must not be regarded as merely an 'economic unit'. It is necessary to distinguish between atheism as a result of a personal choice and atheism imposed by a political system, by unjust means, by moral and even physical pressures. If it is forbidden to constrain anybody to accept faith, it should be also forbidden to constrain a person to profess atheism. Catholics and Protestants may no longer burn one another at the stake, but the wider struggle between Christian and atheist, between the spiritual and the material, though more subtle, is still being fought.

Wojtyla had little experience then with the Western liberal pressures for relaxed stands on birth control, divorce and the ordination of women. Yet he was always committed to the reforms of the Second Vatican Council, particularly the principle of sharing leadership with the bishops, while his deft handling of the strained Church–State relations in Poland proved that he was a real activist on human rights.

Interviewed in 1971 on an investigation into the rights and duties of Catholics in the work of post-Conciliar renewal he said: 'This question ought to be understood as an inquiry into how to carry out the Council's teaching.' This responsibility he qualified under three headings: 1) the witness of the Christian – as one who participates in the redemptive mission of Christ, and as one who values all that is good in nature; 2) the responsibility of Christians to safeguard whatever is authentically human; 3) an attitude of ecumenism – not only in the religious sense, but in a truly Christian social attitude to life. Cardinal Benelli, archibishop of Florence, described Wojtyla's approach to the Vatican Council in the following way: 'His theological attitude is perfectly correct ... What he says comes from his personal conviction. He is the right man at the right time. If there was one man who believed in the Second Vatican Council and had a firm will to carry it out it was Cardinal Wojtyla.'

The openness and zeal for reform which he showed at the Council survived its conclusion and reappeared in even stronger form at the subsequent Synods of Bishops in Rome. Cardinal Wojtyla attended four of the five Synods.

No Polish bishops participated in the first Synod in 1967. Five bishops, including the cardinal from Krakow, were elected to represent the Polish Episcopate. Three of them received passports, but when Cardinal Wyszynski and another bishop were refused permission to leave the country, Cardinal Wojtyla and the remaining members of the delegation also refused to travel, as we have seen. The Polish Episcopate's communiqué as read in all churches accused the authorities of 'seriously restricting the freedom of religion' and disclosed that the regime had rejected the Primate's passport request 'almost at the last moment'.

As we have seen, Wojtyla had travelled to Rome earlier in 1967 for another purpose – to receive the cardinal's red hat. This ceremony was his first real encounter with the world's mass media, involving him in press interviews and photographs. He was, after all, a very young cardinal, only the second from Poland, and still unsure of himself. He was very serious during the interviews, not at all forthcoming, and frequently could not decide whether to grant one or not. All the same, this was a chance for him to get to know many Church dignitaries. As a newly created cardinal protocol demanded that he pay official visits both to those new cardinals who had been given their red hats alongside him, and to some other senior cardinals who happened to be in Rome.

These contacts went off very well. It is interesting that a visit was scheduled to Cardinal Bengsch, the archbishop of Berlin, but that Bengsch unexpectedly arrived at Wojtyla's residence half an hour before the arranged meeting. A bond of friendship has existed between them ever since. Subsequently Wojtyla saw everybody important who was to be seen at the Vatican: Cardinals Cody of Chicago, Krol (of Polish origin) of Philadelphia, Ottaviani, Cicognani, Felici (who in 1978 was destined to announce Wojtyla's election to the Papacy), Villot and many others. He also had long talks with Monsignor del'Acqua, permanent undersecretary of State in the Secretariat of State, Archbishops Casaroli and Montalvo as well as Archbishops Benelli (of Florence), the Yugoslav Seper, Furstenberg, his former professor at the Angelicum, Willebrands of Holland and Palazzini.

According to Bishop Rubin, the secretary general to the Synod of Bishops, the 1969 Synod was the only extraordinary one. Wojtyla was present not as a representative of the Polish Episcopate, but as a nominee of the Pope himself, together with the Primate,

Cardinal Wyszynski. Arguing on the theme of the Pope and the conferences of national Episcopates, Wojtyla spoke out for the primacy of the Pope, on the grounds that this was not in conflict with the principle of collegiality of decision-making. This Synod, according to Bishop Rubin, was a very comprehensive one. It also concerned itself with the problem of the relationship between the Holy See and the national Episcopal Conferences as well as with 'communion between the churches'. Wojtyla became a member of the committee drafting the conclusions of the debates.

Collegiality was for the cardinal from Krakow a very important issue which he argued and interpreted on many occasions. The Synod itself, as he later wrote in *Tygodnik Powszechny*, is a conclusion drawn from the principle of collegiality 'for the needs of our times'. The essence of collegiality is expressed in the words of the Constitution on the Church: 'Together with its head, the Roman Pontiff, and never without this head, the episcopal order is the subject of supreme and full power over the universal Church.' The exercise of this power in conditions of 'dispersal', which is normal for bishops who have their specific local and particular tasks to fulfil, requires that from time to time they supplement their work by acting jointly in the framework of the Synod.

Much attention has been devoted, wrote Wojtyla, to the question whether the Synod of Bishops should have only consultative status (*votum consultativum*) or whether it should be given the constitutive status (*votum deliberativum*) which the Holy Father is in the position to grant. Some people think that withholding this second kind of power diminishes the Synod's importance, the collegial vote being no more than advice for the Head of the Church. It seemed to Wojtyla, however, that this formal aspect was of no decisive importance. The real weight of collegial pronouncements lay precisely in the fact that they were collegial, and in what they said. A vote which was formally only 'advice' for the Head of the Church was at the same time a testimony of the faith and life of all the Churches, expressed by their responsible bishops for the benefit of the whole Church. To the Roman Pontiff such a vote was an immense help. One could say that this process of formation of a collegial vote was a sort of dual confrontation. On the one hand, Wojtyla wrote, it was a confrontation among themselves of the specific views of national Episcopates, out of which grew the most internal and authentic opinion of the Episcopal College. On the other hand, this inter-

nal and authentic opinion became in turn the foundation on which
the Synod as a whole confronted external opinion.

In 1971 Cardinal Wojtyla spoke on two subjects being discussed
by the Synod: the serving priesthood and justice in the world. In
the first speech he based his arguments on his experiences in Poland,
where the priesthood had not forfeited its identity, because it had
work to do and was well prepared for it. 'The State,' he said, 'favours
all the organizations which support atheism in all its expressions,
a programmed atheism, the anti-catechism of the secular world.'
He contrasted the position of Christians, forewarned and forearmed
by the Church, with 'the State, which seeks to create a type of man
subordinated to its own specific ends'. On the delicate subject of
celibacy, Wojtyla maintained it was essential if a priest were to give
himself entirely to the service of others. On the second subject –
justice in the world – Wojtyla argued for freedom of man in all its
aspects, for where there was no freedom there could be no justice.

The cardinal from Krakow came clearly into prominence at this
Synod, and showed his worth. He became known to the cardinals
and bishops of the world with whom he had worked for forty days
at a stretch. His statements, according to Bishop Rubin, were clear
and to the point. He drew people's attention with his fluent command of languages and his youthful energy; he gained prominence
in the various working groups. After 1971 he was elected to the
Council of the Synod Secretariat, receiving in the process an
impressive number of votes: 115 out of 184.

At the 1974 Synod Wojtyla was appointed 'rapporteur' of the
second part of the proceedings on the subject of 'The Gospel in
the Modern World (Part 1 – The Current Situation)'. As Bishop
Rubin sees it, he formulated the principles of evangelization within
the framework of theology in a masterful way. To quote Wojtyla:
'We must go forward, ourselves deeply convinced of the truth which
we are proclaiming.'

One can only speak of authentic evangelization, he argued, when
what is proclaimed and taught is exclusively the Gospel of Jesus
Christ, and not human opinions. Dialogue presupposes and
demands certainty in the faith, without admitting any kind of conformism or doctrinal indifference. Although in multilateral dialogue
there is room for a certain 'opening' of the human spirit and readiness to listen to and understand others, this must nevertheless
always remain in harmony with one's own faith. Such an attitude

in no way diminishes the respect for values inherent in non-Christian religions expressed by Vatican II; it even enhances this respect.

Then Wojtyla raised the issue of ecumenism saying that:

> In preaching Jesus Christ ... the Church by the same token expresses her faith in herself because she is the Mystical Body of Christ ... However, in carrying out this task the Church is always aware that she is only the instrument of this proclamation, not its aim ... This in a particular way leads to evangelization in an ecumenical spirit and concentrating in work and prayer on the aim expressed in the prayer of Jesus 'that they may be one'. The causes of eternal salvation and of the development of man cannot be separated, either in the work of the whole Church or in the lives of individual Christians, for they are closely associated with each other in the order both of creation and of redemption. That is why the dimensions of Christian enterprise which are usually described as 'vertical' and 'horizontal' should not be too sharply set against each other.

And finally, according to Wojtyla, social and economic freedoms, although they are not directly part of the Church's mission, are nevertheless part of the Church's task of furthering the cause of justice and peace in the world.

Summing up the debate, Wojtyla stressed that evangelization does not flourish uniformly throughout the entire world. There emerged at the Synod a 'geography' of conditions for evangelization, and the cardinal argued:

> There is a group of themes that can be bracketed under the term 'indigenization'. It means giving the Church and the process of evangelization in various countries a specific 'native' character, adapted to the needs of specific societies and cultures. This problem came up again and again in the speeches of African bishops ... In the Middle East and the Far East a problem of this kind is their encounter with the great non-Christian religions ... A third group of problems was presented by the bishops of Latin America, the problem of 'liberation' ... theirs is a continent of great social inequalities, and it is only right that the Latin American Church wants to be involved in this struggle for social justice ... The fourth problem is the problem of secularization which confronts the Church in Western Europe and North America, in the former perhaps more than in the latter ... And finally, the fifth and most essential problem is that of religious freedom.

This work on the Synods was in effect the beginning of Wojtyla's rise on the international platform. Other cardinals and bishops began to see him in action at the very heart of the Church; they liked what they saw and admired his intellect.

Archbishop Derek Worlock of Liverpool, who worked with Wojtyla (who, incidentally, has a 'great love for England') after the end of the Vatican Council, and then for ten years on the Council for the Laity, where the two men frequently sat side by side, comments:

He has one of the best brains of any man I have ever met. He is a big man, but his bigness is not a matter of height or width. It is more a question of strength. That is the overwhelming impression; spiritual and moral strength, and strength of intellect. He has a well-ordered and disciplined mind which is undoubtedly the fruit of continuing study and reflection. I know him to be a good listener, often the last one to speak in a discussion. It is his custom to listen carefully and weigh well all the views expressed before delivering his own opinion or answer, deliberately and clearly, sometimes almost in tabulated form.

In debate, as in the rest of his life, he is humble and not self-assertive. But he can, and often does, defend his views resolutely, just as in other respects he will give resolute defence of any rights or freedoms he sees under attack.

He is a man of great principle who has learned to live his beliefs and to proclaim Christian truth even in hostile circumstances. Somehow he has managed to achieve a balance which has enabled him to live and to speak without compromise, and yet apparently without antagonizing unnecessarily or provoking unreasonably those who do not share his views.

In Bishop Rubin's view the 1974 Synod stands out as the best of them all. They did not try – as at previous synods – to prepare a ready-made document within a week or so. Wojtyla and the other rapporteur, the Pakistani Cardinal Cordero, guided the debate and then – together with some other cardinals – took the outline of the document to the Pope for guidance. This was collegiality in practice – the Pope exercising his authority but in accord and consultation with the bishops. The result was one of the best documents ever to come from the Holy See, according to the pro-rector of the English College in Rome, Monsignor Coughlin. It takes in the theology of the Vatican but gives it a new impulse. Wojtyla, along with some others, was instrumental in this exercise.

The 1977 Synod dealt with Catechesis – the problem of religious education. The Primate of Poland was not present and Cardinal Wojtyla led the Polish delegation. Marxist attacks on the Church were referred to by him in harsh terms. The Church was facing 'a growing secularization and planned atheization. Atheism is being imposed like a new religion.' The State, he maintained, must assure full liberty of religious education without any restrictions under any political regime. Wojtyla complained that the Polish authorities were discriminating against believers in public life and prohibiting religious instruction in Polish schools.

In this attack the cardinal was repeating the criticism frequently voiced by the Polish hierarchy. The majority of Poles are believers who support schools by paying their taxes and are therefore entitled to expect the Polish State, whatever the political regime, to provide full, unrestricted freedom of religious instruction. In his view Poland had chosen the best path for catechization, because it had involved young people and families in the task of spreading the Catechism. A Christian, he emphasized, once baptized, should continue to receive religious instruction without a break.

As the most senior cardinal on the Council of the Synod's Secretariat, Wojtyla became its chairman. He summed up their deliberations with great skill, liveliness, humour, calm and clarity, according to Bishop Rubin. The Synod was a platform on which the most outstanding personalities could be assessed and selected. Wojtyla's powers of analysis were widely said to be extremely impressive, as too were all his interventions. The Synods were always the best touchstone of his growing popularity, attended as they were by about sixty cardinals and many archbishops who later became cardinals.

During a period of four to five years his status in the Vatican grew immensely, says Bishop Rubin. By then, the cardinal was a member of several significant Congregations – those for the Eastern Churches, the Clergy, for Divine Service and Catholic Education, for Liturgy. He was also consultant to the Papal Council for matters of the Lay Apostolate. He very often took part in plenary sessions of the various Congregations and he would always make a point of visiting a Congregation whenever he came to Rome on business. Wojtyla's participation in the plenary sessions was very typical of his style. He would listen most attentively to everything being said and would join in himself only towards the end, drawing out and stressing what was particularly valuable and important, and then making his own contribution. Monsignor Coughlin sees

Wojtyla as a profoundly reflective figure, listening extremely carefully to others.

The Polish Church carries a conservative image overall, and its situation is unusual. Some observers in the Vatican consider it as an obedient Church, one that does not have to grapple with secularization problems, wayward theologians, birth control, empty churches, deserted seminaries, or priests straining to get married. Some Catholic liberals argue that while strong Church authority is necessary for survival in Poland, it only causes trouble in the West. Wojtyla was well aware of these tensions even before his election as Pope, and kept abreast of wider Church discussions. Monsignor Peszkowsky, of the Polish-American seminary in Michigan, who has known Wojtyla for twenty-four years, says that while he is interested in the liberal agenda of divorce, celibacy, women priests and the like, he stresses that these problems must be dealt with by 'priestly zeal', by giving individual priests a margin of freedom in applying Church teachings. Archbishop Ignio Cardinale, Apostolic Delegate to Belgium, said of him that he is 'a very devout man, very open ... but very firm in his doctrine'.

At the same time it is interesting that there was tremendous enthusiasm among Polish theological students and priests in Rome when Wojtyla became cardinal in 1967. Those were the times of widespread ferment at universities in Europe and in the United States. These Polish youngsters in Rome had full respect for Cardinal Wyszynski but felt that there should be a much more positive injection of ecclesiology and Vatican Council reforms into the Polish Church. Wojtyla's appointment boosted their morale considerably.

The cardinal from Krakow travelled to Rome more frequently than any other Polish prelate, including Cardinal Wyszynski. In 1970 he led two hundred priests and five bishops, all wartime inmates of German concentration camps, to Rome. On the face of it this was a pilgrimage to celebrate the Golden Jubilee of the Pope's ordination, but this particular pilgrimage paused to remember and pray at Gusen, Mathausen and Dachau. In fact, two anniversaries had coincided: the Pope's Golden Jubilee and the Silver Jubilee of the liberation of the concentration camps, including Dachau, which had been earmarked as the extermination camp for all Polish priests. In St Peter's Basilica, Cardinal Wojtyla preached:

We have come here to testify to our history in the context of our past thousand years. This is the first opportunity we have had since the year of our millennium to bear this witness to our history in such numbers and with such eloquence here, in this holy place. But we have also come here to bear this witness within the context of our own generation; a generation which has been singled out to pass through fire and blood.

In March 1975 Wojtyla, who was being interviewed by Vatican Radio on national preparations in Poland for the current Holy Year, said that the Church hailed the announcement of the Holy Year with great joy. The Year's theme of 'Renewal and Reconciliation' had become an inspiration for many sermons and spiritual exercises. Many pilgrimages to local shrines took place. Official Polish Holy Year pilgrimages to Rome involved 2100 people who came in October 1975 by 220 special flights and were led by Cardinals Wyszynski and Wojtyla.

Cardinal Wojtyla also took part in a meeting between Polish and Italian Catholics in the church dedicated to Our Lady of Czestochowa, and attended the European Bishops' Conference. The meeting, which lasted for five days, with 110 prelates from both the western and the eastern parts of the continent, was the third of its kind held in recent history. Wojtyla was received at a private audience by the Pope before leaving Rome with the last group of pilgrims from his Krakow archdiocese.

Ostpolitik There were, however, less happy occasions between 1969 and 1971 when Wojtyla was deeply involved in the Vatican's Ostpolitik vis-à-vis Poland. From the beginning of 1971 the Church–State dialogue within the country was closely interwoven with the negotiations between Warsaw and the Vatican. The main stumbling block was the Vatican's refusal to recognize the Polish western frontier, and to normalize the Church administration in the newly acquired territories. Both the government and the Episcopate pressed hard for final recognition of the frontiers. Following long-established usage, the Roman Curia had refused, since 1945, to instal as fully-fledged bishops those Polish nominees who acted only as apostolic administrators in these territories, on the grounds that the territorial changes had not been finally recognized in a binding international treaty.

What added insult to injury was the fact that the surviving German ex-holders of the Sees in question continued to be listed in some Vatican publications with their old titles. As long as Bonn con-

tinued to dispute the legal status of the territories the Vatican had
to regard the situation as provisional; it could not appoint bishops
without taking the Polish side in the dispute and thereby damaging
its relations with West Germany. At first there was a hope that the
Vatican would take a decisive step following the West German–
Polish treaty signed in Warsaw in December 1970, but then Archbishop Casaroli the main architect of the Vatican's Ostpolitik,
argued that normalization could only follow ratification of the treaty
by the West German parliament. This was regarded by the Episcopate and the Polish people as 'most unhelpful'. Finally on 28
June 1972, Pope Paul VI appointed Polish resident bishops to
replace the apostolic administrators in the western and northern
territories.

In the new Church–State–Vatican triangle, fresh problems relating to conflicting interests, negotiation aims and the final agreement
itself have all come to the surface since 1972. An accommodation
with the Vatican at the highest level was certainly in the interests
of the Party and the government, since it could lend the Communist
leadership an aura of respectability. If the government itself could
deal directly with Rome, then the image and prestige of the Church
hierarchy were likely to suffer. The Polish leadership might have
tried to settle the normalization of Church–State relations within
the country directly through the Vatican and over the head of the
Polish Episcopate.

The Episcopate was fully aware of this danger, particularly since
Archbishop Casaroli was very keen on coming to terms with the
Polish government, as he had done with Yugoslavia and Hungary.
But the Primate, fully supported by Cardinal Wojtyla and all other
bishops, stressed that before any agreement could be reached his
full approval must be sought, since the Vatican 'is too far away to
fully understand the intricacies of the Church–State relations in
Poland'. Wyszynski thus made sure that there could be no Warsaw–
Vatican normalization before Church–State normalization in the
country, although he was prepared to accept the Vatican's help in
this area. In the circumstances two teams were established to maintain working contacts: the Polish one based in Rome is headed
by a diplomat; Archbishop Luigi Poggi became chief of the Vatican
delegation.

In 1973, after his return from the Vatican, Cardinal Wyszynski
publicly spelled out the conditions under which any normalization

could be achieved in relations with the State. In the first place not only should believers be granted full religious freedom, and have all their human rights respected as guaranteed by the Polish Constitution, but they should also play a full part in the country's social, cultural, and business life. This could not happen until at least some of the outstanding problems were satisfactorily solved. Moreover, the Church had to be free to educate the nation's youth in the spirit of the Gospel. It had an historical right and moral duty to participate in raising the new generation. 'Parties come and go,' the Primate said, 'but the nation remains.'

The government must abandon its attempts to force atheism as well as an alien ideology upon Polish youth by introducing an exclusively 'socialist' curriculum in plans for educational reform, Wyszynski insisted. Discrimination against Catholic citizens in public and professional life had to cease. 'We cannot be pariahs,' he said, 'in the homeland for which we, too, work honestly.' The centuries-old Catholic civilization in Poland had to be given more scope. Catholics and the Church should have access to the mass media and an independent Catholic press should be established. 'Poland should not be a country for non-believers only.' Finally too, the problem of the construction and repair of church buildings without administrative obstructions had to be settled.

While in its Ostpolitik the Vatican Curia played delicately and ambiguously with the idea of collaboration and dialogue with the Communists, Cardinal Wojtyla for one did not need to be told about Communists, nor how much 'pluralism' they are allowed to concede by their ideologies within the countries they rule. The cardinal was guided by two principles. Firstly, no ideological concessions. Secondly, practical, not ideological, cooperation.

In Poland itself, Wojtyla was an advocate of a firmer course in the Vatican's Ostpolitik. For instance, to maintain the fiction that Polish administration of the western territories is still provisional, as Archbishop Casaroli, the architect of Vatican's Ostpolitik, tried to argue (even after the Warsaw–Bonn treaty had been signed in 1970), would have been unrealistic and hostile towards Poland. This was how Cardinal Wojtyla, among others, argued the case.

Many Catholics in Poland felt that in attempting to normalize its relationship with Communist governments the Holy See was giving away too much too soon for too little. Some people even charged that this had only partly to do with overall detente and derived much more from the old Vatican dream of coming to terms with the Moscow patriarchate than from setting out to Catholicize Russia.

It would appear that in October–November 1970 Rome became a battleground where both sides tried to influence the Pope and the Curia on the issue of Polish–West German relations. Both Cardinals Wyszynski and Wojtyla, either together or individually, continued to exert strong pressure on the Vatican, as did Archbishop Doepfner of Munich and Archbishop Hoeffner of Cologne. Neither Wyszynski nor Wojtyla appear to have been received in the Vatican Curia with much enthusiasm. Each had to wait for five days for an audience with the Pope. This must have been particularly irksome for the Primate, in so far as he was received by the Pope only after the latter had met with German bishops from both East and West Germany. Cardinal Wojtyla left Rome for Poland to brief the Polish Episcopate on the talks and to convey a clear idea about the stand of the German Episcopate. But he was back in Rome barely a month after his earlier trip.

In East European Church circles there has been growing dissatisfaction with the Vatican's Ostpolitik on the grounds that the Vatican's conciliatory attitude to the Communist governments of Eastern Europe produced few real improvements in the position of the Churches there, except of course in the special case of Poland. Local Church leaders were often left with the feeling that the Vatican was negotiating over their heads, and sometimes to their disadvantage. The Polish Church, speaking from strength, was able to express its reservations to the Vatican quite openly, making it clear that it did not favour full normalization of Polish–Vatican relations unless its basic demands were met by the Polish authorities. Wojtyla was the most outspoken supporter of this policy.

The Poles finally won the battle in 1972. The main thrust of the Vatican's Ostpolitik slightly but significantly shifted. While the Church has sought to see its mission and vocation recognized, and to be granted freedom to evangelize the nation, it has also shown willingness to maintain a dialogue with the Communists provided they grant the freedom the Church is seeking. This is what the late Pope suggested to the Polish Communist Party leader Gierek during the latter's audience with him. Cardinal Wojtyla was present at the Vatican then, and played an important part in this transformation of relations, which may not quite coincide with the thinking of some Vatican 'experts' on Communist affairs.

For Poland the whole affair obviously involved her relations with Bonn. Here Wojtyla (who was then archbishop) scored a considerable personal success in 1966 by his carefully prepared pastoral letter for his archdiocese, in which he explained the whole background to the famous 1966 letter of conditional 'reconciliation' from the Polish Episcopate to the German bishops. He himself was co-author of the letter, which was strongly condemned at the time by the then Party chief Gomulka, who himself just two years later publicly invited the Bonn government to initiate negotiations with Warsaw.

Cardinal Wojtyla enjoyed very friendly relationships with the West German hierarchy and went to the Federal Republic twice (1974 and 1977) before his official visit with the Polish Episcopate delegation under the Primate's leadership in September 1978. As for reconciliation, 'we still have to work very hard', he said in 1977 in an interview on West German television. He noted that before full reconciliation could be achieved the causes for the tragedies in German-Polish relations had to be given much thought. For him this was a troubling moral problem.

The same attitude was apparent in Cardinal Wyszynski's statements at a press conference in Cologne on the last day of the Polish delegation's visit to West Germany in September 1978. He called the trip a real pilgrimage and appealed for 'cooperation and understanding' between Polish and German Catholics, which should be based on 'fundamental principles of Christian morality'. Discussing Polish–German relations, Wyszynski stated that they should be orientated towards the future rather than 'looking back to the past', although one still had to remember the past in order not to 'perpetuate its mistakes'. The visit, on the Church's initiative, marked a significant turn in Polish–German rapprochement.

One significant aspect of the visit was the warm way Cardinal Wojtyla was welcomed by the West German Episcopate and mass media, who immediately recalled his previous unofficial visits. The German bishops were much impressed by his intellectualism; they admired his deep knowledge of the problems of young people both in the West and in the East. Cardinal Hoeffner, Archbishop of Cologne, found him 'a modest man, of profound piety, strong faith, pastoral devotion and unshakable confidence'.

Yet again, events during the visit showed to what a remarkable degree Wojtyla possesses the ability to concentrate. He was celebrating a mass in Mainz at which Wyszynski was due to deliver a sermon. Without prior notice Wojtyla suddenly learned he would have to reply to a welcoming address by a German cardinal, and explain the sense and the significance of this first official visit as well as give a résumé of relations between the two Episcopates. Bishop Rubin, who was present in Mainz, recalls: 'I was celebrating mass with him and I could see how, at the same time, Wojtyla was thinking hard about his reply. When it came, it was a model of clarity. It came out sentence by sentence, slowly, but with every phrase full of meaning and not a single empty or redundant word.'

Wojtyla often preached without notes, and had to improvise the substance and form of his sermon. 'An excellent sermon,' a priest said on one occasion, 'but what a pity that it took so long.' Yet as Archbishop Poggi remarked once, Wojtyla would 'hack out' the most beautiful forms from his raw material, and fill them with a profound substance.

Pope Paul VI   It may have been for this very reason, according to Bishop Groblicki (vicar general of the Metropolitan Curia in Krakow), that Pope Paul VI invited Wojtyla to deliver retreat sermons for the Holy Father and the Roman Curia in 1976. The late Pope wanted to show the Polish cardinal's abilities to the other cardinals and bishops. A slightly different version comes from Bishop Rubin, the general secretary of the Synod of Bishops in Rome: Paul VI had been looking for a Pole to lead the Vatican retreat for some time, and in 1976 Cardinal Benelli suggested that the Polish Church should itself propose someone for the task. The Polish Episcopate put forward Wojtyla, and the choice was warmly welcomed by the Pope.

The cardinal, who had about two weeks to write the sermons, said to Rubin: 'Do you want me to write a book straight off? Well, here you are.' These were the famous twenty-two Lenten sermons preached in the Vatican. A young priest who knew Wojtyla well, recalls how the cardinal worked on them: 'The main thing he did was to pray; to argue with God, in the best sense, before and during the retreat, from eight to eleven in the morning. He would walk in the Vatican gardens and meditate. "The apostles slept for one hour in the garden of Gethsemane," he said to me, "and we have no way of telling what Christ went through at that time. Yet how many hours have we slept through?"'

It was known that Wojtyla was very close to Paul VI, who willingly listened to what he had to say. The cardinal always had an excellent grasp of the subject in hand, the doctrinal problems of the Church and what the Church lived by and stood for. The Pope, himself an intellectual of considerable calibre, recognized in Wojtyla a kindred spirit. Some well-informed Church sources suggested that the cardinal, in his book *Love and Responsibility*, was one of the inspirers of Pope Paul VI's controversial encyclical *'Humanae Vitae'*. But they add that Wojtyla would want to apply the line of the encyclical less strongly than Paul VI. He would rather stress proper education, they say, and not prohibiton.

It was also known that the Polish cardinal was much closer to the late Pope's way of thinking on the question of relations with the Communist-ruled countries than with the ideas of some of the prelates within the Vatican Curia. He summed up his feelings on this question in an article published in the *Osservatore Romano* in February 1976: 'One can understand that a man may search and not find; one can understand that he may deny; but it is not understandable that a man may have imposed on him the dictum – "it is forbidden for you to believe".' When he was asked whether Marxism could be reconciled with Christianity, Wojtyla replied bluntly: 'This is a curious question. One cannot be a Christian and a materialist; one cannot be a believer and an atheist.'

Thus there is no doubt that the late Pope regarded Wojtyla as an outstanding churchman and intellectual. He saw in the Pole a potential leader, not only in his own country but perhaps on a world stage.

New Horizons Wojtyla's rise to eminence was also due in no small part to his frequent trips abroad. He travelled all over the world, far more so than most of his fellow churchmen. As always in his life there was a manifold purpose in his travels: to see the world and to learn; to meet and talk to people; to attend Church ceremonies and ecclesiastical gatherings; to establish close contacts with foreign Church dignitaries; to establish links with Poles abroad and strengthen their ties with the 'old country'; to preach and to lecture.

Wojtyla has visited most West European countries, and especially Italy, numerous times. He went to Australia to attend the Eucharistic Congress in 1973, and took the opportunity to visit New

Zealand, New Guinea and the Philippines. While he was in the Philippines he met a prominent layman, Jeremias Montemayor, who said of him, 'As he grasps your hand, you immediately feel his great strength, not only of his body but of his character. His eyes tell you of his big pure heart. As he puts his arms around your shoulders you feel his warm compassion, his deep sincerity and his fierce loyalty.'

He has also been a visitor to Canada and the United States (he attended the Eucharistic Congress in Philadelphia in 1976). The friendships, particularly with various bishops and cardinals, cemented during those travels helped him greatly in his pastoral work and in his dealings with the Vatican. Whenever he was abroad Wojtyla was as keen as he was in Poland to be in touch with students, and was frequently seen surrounded by, and working with, groups of young Poles, many in colourful national costumes, listening, discussing, joking and generally enjoying themselves. In Chicago, for instance, he was twice seen strolling around Polish neighbourhoods, and is still remembered there as a warm, deeply spiritual and charismatic personality.

For Wojtyla the Eucharistic Congresses were derived from the importance of the Eucharist in the life of the Church. They are a communal public expression of the manifold needs of mankind and public adoration of the Bread of Life which Christ has given the Church to satisfy this need. The cardinal had participated in such a Congress in Melbourne in 1973, but there he was only accompanied by two bishops. In Philadelphia, on the other hand, the Polish Episcopate was represented in 1976 by a powerful delegation of eighteen bishops under Wojtyla's leadership. At the same time this was a return visit by the Poles following several visits to Poland by American bishops, including Cardinal Krol. These mutual visits are for Wojtyla a particular expression of collegiality which has developed since the Second Vatican Council.

Wojtyla's first visit to Canada and the United States was really the first such transatlantic trip by a leader of the Polish hierarchy for many years. He arrived in Canada as an official representative of Cardinal Wyszynski, and visited Montreal, Quebec, Ottawa, Edmonton, Calgary, Winnipeg, Toronto, Hamilton, St Catherine's and London (Ontario). In each place he paid visits to the local bishops, including the Primate of Canada, Cardinal Roy, and the archbishop of Quebec, and visited many Polish parishes and communities. He also met many Canadian officials. The highlight of his visit was the celebration of the twenty-fifth anniversary of the existence of the Canadian Polish Congress, held in Toronto on 13 September 1969.

At press conferences during his trip he stressed that in Poland, as a predominantly Catholic country, ecumenical problems were not a major issue. On the other hand, 'in Poland people have a clear choice between atheism and Catholicism'. He sounded optimistic about Polish youth. In Toronto Wojtyla observed that more young people get religious instruction in Poland than in Canada, and that they are more 'intellectually convinced' than many Catholics in Western countries. He said that there was a generation gap in Poland as well as in Canada, and that while Polish youth spoke the same language as youth in other parts of the world, there was, at least, no drugs problem. When asked in Montreal whether there had been an improvement in Church–State relations, the cardinal replied cautiously. He was 'happy' to be in Canada, 'to represent Poland, mainly the Church of Poland – but if I say the Church of Poland, then I mean Poland'. On several other occasions he declined to answer such questions, reminding journalists that his mission was religious and not political.

Wojtyla's visit to the United States was different in character to his Canadian one. At his very first press conference in the States the cardinal said that while in Canada he really represented Cardinal Wyszynski, here in the United States he represented himself. He had previously been invited in 1968 by Cardinal Wright of Pittsburgh, but, as he said, the Polish clergy extended the invitation to cover several American cities.

On the whole, the visit was a great demonstration of the attachment of Polish–Americans to their old country and their position in their new homeland, although many non-Polish Americans also greeted Wojtyla and took part in the celebrations.

The purely religious aspect of the visit was highlighted by Wojtyla's visit to Orchard Lake seminary, whose 353 students are all of Polish origin, and by his participation in celebrations in Doyleston, Pennsylvania, where two-thousand people gathered at the national shrine of Our Lady of Czestochowa. Not since the visit of former President Lyndon B. Johnson in October 1966 had there been such preparation for a visitor to the shrine.

In 1973 Cardinal Wojtyla attended the International Eucharistic

Congress in Melbourne at the invitation of the Polish organizations there and of the Australian Catholic hierarchy. He emphasized the ecumenical character of the Congress, since 'this is a continent where so many believers in Christ belong to so many different churches'. While out east Wojtyla established close contacts with the Australian Poles and visited Polish communities both in New Zealand and in New Guinea. But he also found time to make some excursions into the bush.

At the Eucharistic Congress in Philadelphia in 1976 the Polish delegation was numerically the strongest among those from other Communist-ruled countries, and Cardinal Wojtyla took an extremely active part. His public appearances, and his role in leading several major rites and liturgical services before thousands of assembled pilgrims, sometimes assisted by as many as five-hundred concelebrants, earned him high esteem and many honours.

In Philadelphia on 3 August 1976, in what was regarded as a petition for religious freedom throughout the world, the cardinal elaborated on the 'hunger for freedom and justice', stating that everybody had a legitimate right to freedom, self-determination and choice of career, and to act in accordance with his conviction. This 'hunger for freedom', however, remains unsatisfied in a world where old forms of colonialism are merely being superseded by new ones, and laws on freedom, so perfectly formulated in constitutions and laws, still lack actual implementation in real life. In an obvious reference to the relations prevailing in Communist-ruled countries, he then recalled the plight of those who – in spite of the officially-professed freedom of conscience – still remain 'underprivileged', and in some cases persecuted, because of their religious convictions.

Wojtyla's sermon evoked a strong response among the pilgrims and in the world media. For instance, on West German TV Wojtyla emphasized that his compatriots were particularly sensitive to the idea of freedom as a 'basic right' for nations, as well as for individual human beings. He recalled the case of a fifteenth-century Polish university rector who, during the Council of Constance, spoke out openly against the then generally accepted compulsory conversions to the Catholic faith. 'This principle [of tolerance] remains now, six centuries later, as immediate as it was then,' Wojtyla stressed. In his view, the same should apply to present-day institutionalized atheism, which 'must not be forced on anybody'. Queried about his vast audience's reaction to his sermon, the cardinal replied: 'What I have tried to do was to convince Americans that freedom is not only a thing to have and to use, but something one has to reconquer anew every day. In other words, one should use one's freedom while keeping in mind that of other people.'

Prior to joining the Philadelphia celebrations, Cardinal Wojtyla delivered three lectures for English-speaking audiences: at Stevens Point, Wisconsin, on 'the State of Polish Religious Scholarship', at Harvard University on 'Participation or Alienation', and finally at the Catholic University of America in Washington on 'The Auto-teleology of Man'. Auto-teleology is a concept of the cardinal's particular brand of personalism, and refers to the characteristically human drive of man to go beyond his own humanity and to reach the infinity of God.

Dr Jude Dougherty, Dean of the School of Philosophy at the Catholic University in Washington, described Wojtyla as 'a man of power and authority who has a certain presence of command about him. Nothing in the bad sense like ordering people around – but in the sense that you know that given a challenge, he could respond, because he has the ability, intelligence and the courage to respond.' He also won the admiration of Cardinal Baum of Washington, who praised him as 'an intellectual leader in the world ... he has a deep knowledge of classics, scholastic philosophy and relates that to contemporary philosophy'.

The American visit provided an opportunity for the Polish bishops to establish personal contact with the numerous Polish–American community. Wojtyla observed that there is hardly a community so strongly conscious of its links with the 'old country' as the American Poles. The Church is bound to take these circumstances into consideration in extending pastoral help to these people.

After the Congress, Wojtyla together with other bishops visited several Polish communities in Chicago, Detroit, Baltimore, Buffalo and attended a conference at the Polish Seminary in Orchard Lake. On the agenda were problems connected with the programme of current pastoral work in Poland, including the religious education of youth, the lay apostolate, and other Church-related topics. As Cardinal Wojtyla recalled in his address, the Church in Poland is 'not waging any political struggle', neither is it the 'instrument of some other people's policy'. To fulfil its specific mission, the Church has, however, to maintain its independence. The current trend towards the normalization of relations between the Holy See and the Polish government is viewed with 'due respect'. Nevertheless, he said, nothing could excuse the bishops from fulfilling the duties that confront them as a result of 'Polish reality', i.e. a 'State policy based on atheistic principles'.

Not only did Cardinal Wojtyla travel more than most Catholic prelates ever do, but he also established many more worldwide contacts. There is perhaps only a handful of Church dignitaries he has not met in all the countries he has visited.

Despite all this there were occasional upsets. Not in Philadelphia, however. In the city of Brotherly Love he would assemble all the bishops in the morning and then in the evening to discuss the day's proceedings, plan the programme for the next day and to outline a common policy with them. He was a great believer in such consultations. But, unfortunately, during the visit to West Germany in 1978, the members of the Polish Episcopate's delegation were housed in separate buildings and it proved impossible for the cardinal to organize similar daily meetings. He was very unhappy about that.

More and more cardinals and bishops had come from abroad to see him in Krakow in recent years, among them Cardinals Cody of Chicago, König of Vienna, Krol of Philadelphia (Chairman of the American Bishops' Conference), even Archbishop Casaroli, and many others. He has had widespread contacts with the Church in Africa, and has corresponded widely with black bishops and missionaries. They would often come to visit him in Krakow, perhaps more frequently than other churchmen, and discuss missionary matters.

All Roads Lead to Rome　Wojtyla's participation in the Vatican Council and the Synods of Bishops, his frequent visits to Rome, his interventions on Poland's behalf in the Vatican Ostpolitik, participation in so many Congregations, activities in some Curia departments, travels abroad and contacts established in foreign countries – all this gave him a greater acquaintance with the breadth of the Church's existence and a toehold on the inner workings of the Roman Curia. That being the case, it was perhaps not surprising that when the world suddenly found itself without a Pope, Wojtyla's name should have come to mind.

Whenever he went to Rome he stayed at the Polish College (Pontificium Collegium Polonorum), in one of Rome's tree-lined residential districts; the college stands almost on top of one of the seven hills. Some students and priests at the college recall the many days spent with the cardinal. He often arrived by the morning train and immediately made his way to some meeting or other. His time was limited and he was always in a hurry. He would frequently return to Krakow immediately after the meeting was over.

Once a number of Polish theological students went to the station to meet Wojtyla. He greeted each one of them in a simple, straightforward manner. He did not lunch with them at the College because he was already due at a conference; but he came to the refectory for supper and extended a personal greeting only to those whom he had not met at the station. He knew all the Polish students at the Angelicum Pontifical University by name, including those who were not from his archdiocese, and was interested in their work and progress. At the Polish college they used to arrange name-day parties – a little wine and orangeade. On the first occasion, they debated for a long time whether to invite the cardinal. In the end they did. Since then he has always attended. In 1968 he was made an 'honorary collegian'. Very pleased with this honour, Wojtyla organized a big reception for all the students.

He was a very straightforward person they said, calm with a great sense of humour, gentle and, at the same time, direct. When he stayed in the College all the telephones would be engaged. He met people, helped them, sorted things out for them and personally involved himself in their everyday concerns. Wojtyla would often go to the Vatican Radio to broadcast to Poland in their Polish programmes. A priest who introduced him to broadcasting says that the cardinal was very attentive when being given instructions in microphone technique. Moreover he willingly deleted sentences from his script when asked to do so, or would shorten his text when it was too long. Nor did he get angry when told that this or that sentence had to be rewritten because it just did not lend itself to broadcasting – radio language being specific and different from the written word.

Over the years he became very much at ease with journalists and broadcasters of any nationality. At a dinner at the home of one of his Polish friends in Rome, three Italian TV journalists were desperate to film an interview with Wojtyla. He cleverly but subtly evaded the pressure by saying that he carried his bishop's crozier only on behalf of the Polish diocese and not on behalf of the Italian television services. 'Let the Italian bishops do that job,' he said. 'Very, very shrewd,' one of the Italian journalists remarked, but Wojtyla just smiled.

In the College, where he stayed, he would go to the chapel – a modern, bright building, not very big, but pleasingly arranged – after supper, kneel down near the small organ in a dark corner of the last row, and pray silently. The students used to enter the chapel on tiptoe. When he did not have conferences to attend, Wojtyla would go up on to the highest terrace on the College roof and walk up and down alone with his breviary. He had the most splendid view of the whole eternal city with all its towers, spires, palaces and ancient buildings; a view of eternity. During hot summers, he would go down to the College garden, pull a small table into the shade of a tree and read.

In 1978 the young rector of the College was in Turin staying with the Salesian Fathers. He recounts a story told him by one of the priests: 'A cardinal was here a few days ago: a Polish Cardinal – I can't remember his name, I know he was from Krakow – but what a lesson he gave us all. He asked for the church to be opened, because, he said: "Today's Friday and on Friday I always follow the stations of the Cross."'

The relationship between Wojtyla and the students was always very straightforward: they never called him 'Your Emminence' but simply 'Cardinal'. He stayed at the College on and off over the space of a dozen years after he became an archbishop, and occupied rooms which they used to call 'the Cardinal's Apartment'.

He loved to have guests, and would always be inviting somebody round, such as other cardinals with whom he was working during the various synods. Cardinal Luciani came too. When Luciani had been elected Pope John Paul I, Wojtyla would point out the chair in which he had sat. Before each conclave he would celebrate mass with the students and would preach a short sermon.

Wojtyla would rise earlier than the rest of the priests and students because at seven in the morning he was already celebrating mass in the chapel. After that he would come down to have breakfast in the refectory (a simple oblong room with two long tables and a high table at right-angles at one end), or he would leave for a conference or else work in his 'apartment'. During lunch he would only hold social conversation – no shop-talk – and he would speak with everyone at the table. After the meal he would be out on the terrace with his breviary or in the garden at a table with a book. He would always come back for supper, then back to his breviary and prayers in the corner of the chapel. Money did not exist for him. The sisters bought him a beautiful book-rest, so that he could write while sitting in an armchair. He gave it away to someone and would write in his armchair with a piece of cardboard beneath the paper.

When Wojtyla could spare some time he would go with young priests and students on long walks, hitch-hiking to the beach, or skiing. He made many visits to Mentorella, some forty kilometres from Rome in the Prenestine mountains, on the 1218-metre-high peak of Guandagnolo. Depending on the season he would either climb the mountain or go skiing there. On the summit of the hill stands the shrine of St Eustace, whose history goes back to the first century. According to tradition, St Eustace saw a vision of Christ and died for his faith during the persecution of Christians. What remains today is a small church with a Roman façade and two windows dating back to the twelfth century. A modest monastery stands nearby.

Today five Polish priests guard the church's treasure, a beautiful twelfth-century wooden statue of the Virgin Mary with an infant Jesus on her knees. Cardinal Wojtyla's most recent visit there was on 7 October 1978, only nine days before his election, when he walked the steep twelve kilometres from the village of Capranica Prenestina to the hilltop to pray at the shrine.

6

Cardinal Wojtyla Speaks

Church–State Relations at Home The vicissitudes of relations between Church and State were frequently and often sharply reflected in Cardinal Wojtyla's sermons. At a time when the Catholic Church faces hostile atheism in many parts of the world and sceptical indifference in others, Wojtyla's experience in Poland has a dramatic relevance to its role in the last quarter of this century. He has had to withstand all the rigours of Communist pressure on the Church, to defend its faith, to try to reassert its rights, and, under the leadership of the Primate of Poland, to restrain the most ardently faithful congregation in the world from any rash move that might bring new upheavals. In this he has been so successful that the Polish government has come to accept the Catholic Church as an unofficial loyal opposition.

At a time when the demand for human rights is heard from almost every corner of the world, Cardinal Wojtyla has been their outspoken champion in Poland. But at the same time, and without any sacrifice of principles, Wojtyla has sought prudent accommodation with the government in practical matters, in accordance with the guidelines laid down by Pope John XXIII. Though his personal experience of dealing with Communists in power has doubtless commended itself for one reason or another to sections of informed opinion in the West, Catholics in Eastern Europe were more likely to be heartened by Wojtyla's bringing to the Vatican's much discussed and, to some, suspect Ostpolitik a thoroughly realistic practical assessment of how far cooperation between Marxists and Christians was possible without confusing the faithful.

All the Church's demands and complaints against some Polish government measures came under the common denominator of human rights and basic individual liberties. Over the years, Wojtyla consistently opposed official, social and political discrimination against believers in public life. In 1962 he accused the leadership

of violating the human rights of the Catholic population by restricting religious education for children. At the time the Communist
regime had not only withdrawn its earlier agreement to allow the
teaching of religion in schools (after the so-called Polish Spring in
October 1956) but had begun to create many difficulties in the religious instruction of children outside schools at the so-called catechetic points.

During the celebrations of the millennium by the Church in
Poland the Communist authorities did their best to oppose and
obstruct the ceremonies, regarding them as political demonstrations. In Krakow in May 1966 Cardinal Wyszynski referred to St
Stanislaw, an early medieval Polish bishop – another Thomas
Becket – who clashed with the king, and was killed. Appropriately
enough, Wyszynski said that the Catholic Church had been involved
in the fate or Poland for ten centuries and was just as deeply involved
today. It was the then Archbishop Wojtyla who made the point by
welcoming the Primate with the words: 'You have received blows
to the head and the heart. Such blows reach through the past to
St Stanislaw himself.'

Years later (on 8 May 1977) Cardinal Wojtyla returned to the
subject in his pastoral letter, stressing the principle of the freedom
of man:

St Stanislaw has become the patron saint of moral and social order
in the country ... He dared to tell the king himself that he was bound
to respect the law of God. The age-old veneration of St Stanislaw is,
in fact, a confession of the truth that moral law is the foundation of social
order. He was also the defender of the freedom that is the inalienable
right of every man, so that the violation of that freedom by the State
is at the same time a violation of the moral and social order.

On the 600th anniversary of his own Jagellonian University in
Krakow, Wojtyla recalled the times of his secret underground
studies during the Nazi occupation:

This thirst for truth asserted itself magnificently in the years of the
occupation in the form of secret tuition organized by the University.
Eight hundred students benefited from it. This was impressive evidence,
probably unique in the history of universities, of a striving for truth that
was not afraid of anything, of a readiness to fight and suffer for truth.
I mention this because I myself am a product of this secret tuition.

But Wojtyla himself had not even been invited to the ceremonies.

'Proud, small and arrogant men,' Cardinal Wyszynski said, 'came and ordered that not a single mention of the Church and its work must be made at these celebrations.'

Then came March 1968, and massive student demonstrations in Warsaw and other Polish cities flared up with demands for freedom of expression and abolition of censorship. They were brutally put down by the militia. Jews were made scapegoats for the students' and intellectuals' rebellion and were hunted and expelled from the country. For the first time in Polish history, antisemitism had become official government policy. Cardinal Wojtyla went on record as strongly condemning the evils of antisemitism and prodded the bishops to support persecuted intellectuals and students. In Krakow he firmly opposed the expulsion of the remnants of Polish Jewry from the country of their birth. And at the Vatican Council he spoke positively and constructively about the declaration on the relations of the Church with non-Christian religions, including Judaism ('*Nostra Aetate*'). In 1969, during his visit to Boston, Wojtyla once more invoked the need to 'safeguard human rights and personal as well as social perfection'.

Poland is the only country within the Soviet orbit which has twice thrown out the Communist Party and government leadership by massive and dangerously strong pressure from below: in 1956 when Gomulka took over and in December 1970 when he was eliminated politically and replaced by the present Party leader, Gierek. Gierek's openings to the Church were welcomed, with reservations, by the hierarchy, including Cardinal Wojtyla. The conditions of the modus vivendi outlined by the Church's hierarchy (see Chapter 2) frequently had the imprint of Wojtyla's mind and inspiration.

All the while he was growing in stature and growing politically. His sermons and pastoral letters were becoming increasingly outspoken while maintaining a calm and restrained tone. This was certainly true in the years 1976–8, when Wojtyla frequently criticized the government for its treatment of dissenters, workers, students and intellectuals. He strongly defended their rights to publicize their complaints and to freely express their opinions. It was in June 1976 that massive strikes and demonstrations by the workers led to the authorities having to capitulate and change their policies.

Significantly, very few excerpts from Wojtyla's sermons were published in the independent Catholic press because of heavy censorship. They only appeared in the Episcopate's internal bulletin, which thus provides a wealth of material concerning his thoughts on contemporary Poland. Perhaps even more interesting is the fact that while these sermons analyse local Polish issues they nevertheless have a universal significance. Similar situations obtain in many other countries in the world, under different political systems.

When in 1973 the Party disclosed its plan to reform the educational system by injecting 'socialist principles' into the curricula the Church condemned the move instantly. Cardinal Wojtyla was quoted as saying that he would 'set all possible wheels in motion to bring about a victory for freedom of conscience'. The education of the young must not be one-sided, and had to take into account the traditions of the nation and its Christian culture.

'The situation in Poland today demands a spiritual defence of the faith,' Wojtyla said, and recalled how in a recent pastoral letter the Polish bishops had accused the official atheization programme of making use of clandestine methods which on the surface looked neutral or even positive. Of course, everyone was in favour of the extension of education facilities as envisaged in the reform of the schools. But when the curricula and timetables proposed were such that they left the children no time whatever for religious instruction, the question arose whether a praiseworthy concern for education was the only purpose of the reform. The faithful could not afford to accept this programme of forced laicization. They had to stand up in defence of their faith and of their children (January 1976).

About a month later Wojtyla wrote an article in the *Osservatore Romano* headlined 'The Truth about Man'. In it he called for genuine freedom of conscience and religion, as embodied in the UN Charter of Human Rights and, more recently, in the final act of the Helsinki Conference. It was his opinion that believers in Poland had been and were still being treated as 'second-class citizens' and given a 'position of inferiority' in public life, with the majority of them barred from holding public office. As long as one single social group – 'no matter how well deserving' – was able to force upon the whole nation an ideology that 'ran counter to the convictions of the majority' and as long as, in an eminently Catholic country, atheism was being made the 'foundation of national life', the situation could hardly be deemed satisfactory.

Wojtyla has expressed similar views on various occasions, as for example during his visit to the Vatican in December 1975. According to the unofficial Catholic daily *L'Avvenire* he discussed the

plight of the Polish Church at a symposium in Milan and devoted
the last part of his address to an examination of the rights of men
and nations to religious freedom. This freedom was best defined,
he stated, by the Church's right to appoint bishops, to teach and
educate in accordance with national and religious traditions, and
to contribute in its own way to maintaining 'social and human
order'. Lack of such rights was denounced as 'spiritual slavery', by
no means less than physical slavery and requiring much Christian
courage to be effectively countered.

This Christian courage had to be shown by everybody and everywhere, particularly in schools at all levels. On Christmas Day 1977,
Wojtyla preached:

We hear sometimes that there is to be a second Poland. But there is
only one Poland, and this second one, if it is to be Poland, must spring
from the first. It may not deny any element of our national and cultural
heritage ... The various proposals we hear concerning education, the
teaching of history and literature make us ask with apprehension whether
the aim is really that we should remain ourselves.

Schools, said Wojtyla, were most important. They belonged to
the people as a whole and therefore:

They must not be used for the propagation of ideas which are at vari-
ance with the convictions of the majority of Poles, that is, against the
convictions of believers. We are often approached and asked to help combat the spreading immorality. But in that case the Church must first be
given the necessary means ... including access to the radio and television.

In September 1977 the cardinal had taken to task the author of
an article in the locak Krakow press who argued that there is freedom of religion and freedom of conscience in Poland, that everything that is going on in Poland is, in fact, in full harmony with
the teaching of the Second Vatican Council! At the same time, however, the author argued that this alleged freedom was consonant
with the right of the State to become engaged in the propagation
of a single ideology. 'What curious dialectics!' Wojtyla exclaimed,
and concluded his analysis with the bitter remark: 'It looks as if
we were being given to understand that indeed we do count as instruments of production but we do not count as human beings, as
co-authors of the reality of contemporary Poland.

In Cardinal Wojtyla's view, teachers clearly have an obligation
to educate Polish children in the same spirit as their Catholic

families would teach. But teachers are also instruments of authority. Delivering a sermon in July 1978, he said:

If a school and its teachers are to remain true to the self-evident principles of justice and truth, then you cannot tie that school to biased one-sided ideas. Schools must not be regarded as an instrument serving a particular viewpoint and a particular orientation. One cannot allow schools in Catholic Poland to become the tools of atheization. This is contrary to Poland's national interest, because that interest should reflect all that harmonizes with Polish history and with Polish culture. Poland's national interest also demands that given our present-day realities, both human rights and those of the nation should be respected.

It should not be required of our teachers, the overwhelming majority of whom are, as children of this nation, themselves believers, that they should by virtue of their position and profession become advocates of a viewpoint they do not share. You cannot expect such an act of hara-kiri to be inflicted on human conscience and on human personality. You cannot expect a person who teaches and hands down truth to himself live in falsehood. For this goes against the dignity of Man, and does not suit our Polish national interest ... The future of our country depends on whether the people we are now teaching in our schools will be independent, spiritually mature and socially responsible.

Wojtyla attached the greatest importance to proper education at universities and created special university chaplaincies to secure 'a full Christian training' of students. In October 1978 he preached:

The years of higher studies are of particular importance in the development of a young personality ... The faith of an educated man must nowadays be particularly well formed and mature ... There is a danger of religious illiteracy.... Higher education must not be confined to narrow specialization which overlooks essential problems of the nation, the modern world and the Church. In Poland the Church has always been closely associated with the national culture, which from the very beginning bears a very strong Christian imprint.

The young seek anxiously for the truth – that was Wojtyla's motto – both in schools and at the universities. He said in his homily at Jasna Gora:

It is necessary for new generations of Poles to get to know the whole truth of the nation's past. We hear sometimes that boys and girls in school do not want to learn history. Apparently they refuse to accept what they are being taught. A healthy instinct, a sense of truth, makes them turn away from history lessons which give them a distorted picture of the nation's past, distorted according to certain well-known prescriptions. They look for the truth elsewhere. (July 1978.)

To seek the truth and to transmit it to the nation as a whole was another of Wojtyla's preoccupations. Here the problem of the mass media arose. The important thing in our dialogue with the State, he said to an American journalist friend, is access to the mass media and the teaching of religion in schools.

Few prelates are perhaps as aware of the importance of the mass media in the contemporary world as is Wojtyla, particularly in countries where information is so much one-sided. The Polish Episcopate has asked for media access many times, and Wojtyla insisted on it in the strongest possible terms. 'The Press lies!' was a slogan shouted at many upheavals in post-war Poland. And this was also true at the time of the June 1976 riots (see Chapter 2).

Cardinal Wojtyla summarized the problem in at least three of his sermons, in which he stressed that moral authority, not violence, should be expected from those in power. In January 1977 he declared:

We want the climate of truth to become that of our social life. We want to see a true picture of ourselves in newspapers, in the radio, in television. We do not want an artificially contrived truth, a manipulated public opinion. But what we read and what we hear through the media is not a true picture of ourselves – as if Poland were an atheistic country. All sorts of people have the right to address us by way of radio and television, but the sick can never hear mass being broadcast or televised. We do not want an authority based on police batons.

In a sermon preached in December 1977, recalling that the right to know and to tell the truth has its roots in the Christian tradition, Wojtyla said:

Every man is called to be a witness to the truth. In the right kind of social order this calling is respected, every man has the right to speak his mind, no one is forced to hide truth in some sort of underground, no one is denied the necessary means of expressing this truth, and truth is not manipulated in the interest of one particular set of ideas which is foisted upon society to the exclusion of others ... In our times, when the mass media have become such important means of communicating ideas, the Church must also have access to them. It is inadmissible that these means should be used exclusively in the service of one point of view, largely opposed to the views and convictions of the majority of the population. They must become open to all ...

There was unmistakable support for opposition groups which have been growing in the country since June 1976, largely among young people. In his sermon on Corpus Christi in June 1977 Cardinal Wojtyla added to this theme:

The profound truth felt by each individual, especially by the young, must be respected. The young most certainly cannot be tailored to schemes fashioned from above. Our Polish press must take this into serious consideration. The press cannot, as happens in many countries of the world, just behave as an instrument for manipulating public opinion. Man is a thinking animal; man seeks the truth. And the Pole has more than a thousand years of truth searching behind him, and that provides a particular sort of maturity, even for the apparently immature or the only recently matured. If men read in the papers what they know to be a falsehood, they feel bitter on account of being made to live a lie, a forgery; and fearful lest a lie is told about them everywhere – about all Poles, their deeds and their attitudes.

For example, if someone were to base their knowledge and opinions on Poland and present-day Poles on what they read in our daily press, a press which has been described as an instrument of State, then they might well be surprised if they found themselves here today at the Corpus Christi procession: how does this tally with what one reads in the papers?

On the other hand, Wojtyla frequently praised the part played by few independent Catholic publications, including *Tygodnik Powszechny*, which, as he said, became over the years 'a particular platform for a test of strength of the Polish Catholic lay community'. He demanded at least one truly Catholic daily paper, since in the present situation the number of Catholic publications represents only a tiny proportion of the 'mass of publications' controlled by those who are opposed to Christian teachings.

While dealing with all these subjects Wojtyla voiced frequent and sometimes strongly worded complaints about the difficulties which the authorities deliberately put in the way of children and students at holiday camps to prevent them attending religious instruction; about harassment of people who offered their homes for religious classes; about the fact that some workers are required to work on Sundays. 'Sunday belongs to us,' he said, 'and no one has the right to deprive us of our Sunday. We have the right to demand the humane organization of work.' (May 1978.)

However strongly worded and outspoken some of Wojtyla's sermons might have been, he and the whole Episcopate unfailingly counselled moderation in times of potential danger, while at the same time standing up in defence of workers who demonstrated and of those who helped them. This was the case after the June 1976 upheaval, when during a sermon in Krakow in December Wojtyla said:

We cannot afford to be irresponsible, for we are in a difficult geographical position. That is why every Pole is charged with a special responsibility, which in present times is even more special. This past year has not been an easy one. From the very first months of the year we had to take up a fight for the basic truths of our existence as a nation and as a State. We had to repeat again and again that the State exists for the nation, and not the other way round. After so many struggles, so many wars on various fronts, after so much suffering, this nation deserves to be free and independent. We must be extremely watchful not to squander this arduous but great inheritance, or let it be squandered. As this year comes to a close we have to pray more than ever for those who suffer. Since the end of June the Polish Episcopate has repeatedly demanded that those who merely stood up in defence of their livelihood and of tolerable material standards should not be punished for that ... And we must go on praying that our country be a land of real freedom, true justice and respect for human rights.

However, many of the problems between Church and State remained unresolved, and the erratic policy of the Communist Party, with its often conflicting decisions seemingly taken at random, did not help to stabilize the situation. Wojtyla took a rather sombre view of events in the country in a sermon delivered in June 1978:

There is a marked lack of sensitivity, and concern for others; fostering one's own career at other people's expense; undermining one another's position; a widespread sense of mistrust. Instead of a growing community spirit there is increasing social atomization. In the name of socialization people are herded into ever vaster industrial establishments and housed in multi-storey tower blocks where they are hermetically separated from each other. It is not only the walls that separate them, it is the whole atmosphere of distrust, indifference and alienation. In such an atmosphere the human heart withers. It is a development that goes against everything that is best in the Polish tradition.

Then there was the problem of discrimination against believers within the context of the human rights issue, of which Wojtyla was the most forceful champion. In December 1977 he declared:

The rights of Man are an essential part of being human, and God, by becoming man, confirmed the dignity of being human. That is why they cannot be arbitrarily circumscribed. No one can say: you have these rights because you are a member of such and such a nation, race, class or party; and to you they are denied because you do not belong to this nation, race, class or party ... Every man by virtue of being man has a right to social advancement in the framework of his community. And every man has the duty to shape the life of the whole community by promoting justice and love, not by factional struggles, in the name of a single class. Every man born on this Polish soil is by this very token a child of the Polish motherland. It is impermissible to tell anyone that he or she is a lesser kind of Pole than any other Pole.

And in another sermon in September 1978:

It is intolerable that public institutions which belong to the whole nation should be used for the benefit of only one philosophy, of a single political orientation. It is intolerable that membership of a political organization should be the price people have to pay for their existence, for their place in society. It is intolerable that people should be divided into a privileged and an unprivileged section according to a political criterion.

For Wojtyla, each individual Pole is responsible for the whole nation:

It is unthinkable that a man charged with that responsibility should squander his humanity in any wanton form of behaviour, in drunkenness, careerism, pursuit of material gains, cheap conformism and atheism. All these are despicable forms of slavery, whereas a truly responsible life is a life of freedom. It is a freedom that originates in God and demands, therefore, at all times an uncompromising respect for truth. Respect for truth can be a costly virtue, but it is armed with that virtue that Poland has come through her first millennium, and only armed with that virtue can the nation enter the second millennium. (May 1978.)

While Cardinal Wojtyla was always in the forefront of the struggle for human rights not only in his own country but all over the world, he never spoke out so strongly for these rights as in 1976–8. His appeals were linked with the cause of the Church, but the significance of his words in secular, political terms could not be ignored. This was his greatest battle, which he fought for the restoration of intellectual and personal freedoms in Poland which were guaranteed by the country's Constitution in all spheres of human life but seldom applied in everyday practice.

What, for instance, constitutes genuine religious freedom? Wojtyla defined this in March 1978 as 'the freedom for Christ to be openly with every man in all circumstances of his life'. He went on to expand on this in the following words:

What is at stake is that this freedom should be available in every nation, in every state, on all continents, in any political system. And moreover that a man who walks with Christ should be free to acknowledge his companion, and not have to pretend that Christ is not with him. It is a denial of religious freedom when you are told, for instance, that you may be with Christ in church, but you are not allowed to take Him with you to school because the school must be secular. In this way man is artificially split in two. And that is inadmissible.

After the June 1976 riots the Party leadership played for time in lieu of taking firm action. Nationwide frustration was becoming more and more widespread, while various opposition groups were openly growing in strength, protesting against injustices, harassment and reprisals, and busy outlining programmes of change within the existing system. The so-called 'flying university', a series of lectures given in private homes by well-known academics, created an alternative educational system for university students to supplement the official distorted and strictly 'socialist' curricula taught at higher schools.

In May 1977 a Krakow university student active in the opposition movement was found dead. Murder according to the students. Accidental death, the authorities maintained. In any case thousands of students attended a requiem mass and later gathered around Wawel Castle with black banners in a candlelight procession demanding punishment of those responsible for the 'murder'. They formed an alternative students' organization, because, as they said, the official students' association did not represent their interests.

It was then that the whole concept of human rights was carefully analysed in Wojtyla's two sermons on Corpus Christi day in 1977 and 1978. In May 1977 thousands of young people, mostly students, thronged the streets of Krakow, led by their bishops and their cardinal during celebrations in homage to St Stanislaw. As the cardinal spoke in the open air in defence of civil rights and against repressive measures, a military jet circled above the square in an effort to make him inaudible This was greeted with derisory laughter from the crowd and by applause when the cardinal looked up and smilingly greeted the 'uninvited guest'.

In June 1977 Wojtyla gave the most comprehensive picture of what had to be done in the field of human rights if justice and peace were to prevail:

Proof is urgently required that human rights and the rights of citizens are being honoured, because the problem seems to be escalating in the world at large and in our own community. These rights are indispensable. Human rights, rights of the individual, and in their wake, the rights of communities – the Church is just such a body in the land of Poland – are indispensable. They cannot be given in the form of concessions. Man is born with them and seeks to realize them in the course of his life. And if they are not realized or experienced, then man rebels. And it cannot be otherwise, because he is man. His sense of honour expects this.

Thus it is certainly in the interests of all authorities everywhere in the world, no less than in Poland or in Krakow, to appreciate the need, to respect human rights. The man who feels that he is being deprived in this respect is ready to commit any act. He is prepared to make many sacrifices! He cannot cease being a man, a Pole or a Christian: he cannot simply stop being any of these things.

And it is impossible to resolve these problems by means of oppression. Police and prisons provide no answer either. They only raise the price that will ultimately have to be paid. The solution does not lie with expanding police organizations and State Security departments. There is only one road to peace and national unity, and that is through unfettered respect for the rights of man, for the rights of citizens and Poles.

The authorities do not possess a mandate merely to dominate, and to use those means at their disposal solely for purposes of domination. Their duty is to guard the rights of man, of the citizen, of the Pole, and of the Christian, and to see that their rights are fully respected! These matters cannot be resolved otherwise ...

The Church in Poland seeks no authority other than to bear witness to the truth about God and about man ... Man is not simply a body; he also possesses a soul. This has perhaps been forgotten in the face of materialism. The situation must be put right at the earliest possible moment ... The man who follows God, who speaks the truth, must be allowed to enjoy a proper place in the community, and must not be constricted, shackled or put into a straitjacket ...

The student body – the mature and independent youth – shoulder special responsibility for the country's and the Church's future. Their future responsibilities are various – they are social, political, cultural and religious. They are our future. That is why one should be pleased when given reason to believe that the young are not only jovial, even unruly, but that they have serious thoughts on life and matters of a general social nature as well as of a personal nature. At this point I must return to the events of May. Everyone was pleased that the day had passed and ended peacefully. The students of Krakow assembled in the evening at the foot of Wawel Castle and sang the national anthem. It is natural that they should sing thus, for Poland's destiny after all lies in their hands. But they also sang a second hymn, a church hymn – 'Lord, Redeem for us a free Poland'. [This hymn has strong national connotations and is frequently regarded as Poland's second national anthem.]

Equally significant is the fact that the students chose to assemble together and that they chose peace, rather than the uproar of an annual 'juvenalia'. It shows that the young are capable of thinking about fundamental issues such as the great mystery of death, social justice and peace, the rights of the individual and of a nation, and feel a responsibility for the great national heritage of our Polish people ...

If the press wishes to be taken seriously it must not misrepresent this society. The press has a responsibility towards the nation and the individual, and not only towards a single institution. Thus we make a grave appeal to the press to join all of us who care what happens to our homeland, in serving the rights of man, and the nation, rather than following a policy of selecting one-sided information opinions and attitudes. It is particularly hurtful when this biased attitude affects someone who is unable to defend himself ... But unfortunately the press is a monopoly and it is biased ... I plead all this in the name of ancient customs and in the name of our Polish traditions of toleration. Nobody will lose by this. Certainly not the authorities, because authorities that can boast of living the truth are strong; truth begets strength, at least it does so in our culture and our national tradition.

A year later, in June 1978, again on Corpus Christi day in Krakow, Cardinal Wojtyla elaborated on the theme of human rights, social justice and peace:

Our prayers for peace and justice in the modern world and in our Polish land are prayers for Mankind and for each and every man. They are prayers for human rights; rights which cannot be tailored to fit a particular system nor a particular doctrine; rights which have to be seen in the truth of Man's greatness and Man's freedom. And these rights cannot be taken away from him! Especially when one declares support for those selfsame rights; especially when one guarantees them. We, therefore, pray for justice in our land, that human rights may be recognized on the basis of the Truth that is Man.

... The problem of peace must be seen as the problem of Man. We believe that unless the world matures into recognizing a man's worth, unless it becomes convinced that you cannot take away a man's innate and irrefutable rights, cannot place restrictions on him, cannot trample on him, cannot imprison him for his beliefs, cannot commit acts of terrorism against him such as leave the world trembling; unless all this matures, peace itself is greatly endangered.

Ours is a difficult and glorious past, a past which wrung the tears of whole generations; a past in which generations bled and were shackled. Our country is so much the dearer to us since it was bought at the cost of so many generations.

We shall not tear ourselves away from our past! We will not allow our past to be torn from our souls. It is the essence of our identity even today. We want our young people to be familiar with the truth and history of our nation. We want the inheritance of our Polish culture to be passed on without any deviations, to new generations of Poles. A nation lives by the truth about itself! And it has a right to attain that truth. Above all it has a right to expect that truth from those who teach. Because we love that truth! And let no one dare to separate us from our love for the fatherland; our love for Poland. I include all Poles without exception in this prayer for our country ... but especially our youth, because we can see the great dangers confronting it.

This was Wojtyla's testament for Poland and her rulers, delivered before he knew that his intimate concern for his beloved country would of necessity be reduced in the light of greater responsibilities. Not only did workers, students intellectuals and dissenters enjoy his moral support, but he helped them in many practical ways. One of his last acts before becoming Pope was to lend his support to the 'flying university' in a rather special and different way. Quoting the Episcopate's letters of March and September 1978 (see Chapter 2), he set up five annual academic courses under the roofs of five Krakow churches as part of the Church's ministry. The concept is a broad one designed to supplement official university education. It is carefully planned, and the courses deal with literature, philosophy, social sciences, history and Biblical theology – subjects either ignored or distorted in the State's institutes for higher learning.

Wojtyla's outspoken sermons, and the fact that he specifically protected students in situations such as that following the mysterious death of the student activist in May 1977, won him a large following

among the young, even among atheists. A male student in Krakow
says: 'In May 1977 there was a strong possibility that all of us would
find ourselves in prison. It was therefore all the more important
that Cardinal Wojtyla spoke out and entrusted the students to the
care of the city. He spoke out boldly and openly. He is the representative of a fighting and struggling Church, which is a symbol,
a sign for the whole world.'

For another male student from Krakow the Church is the only
institution that can defend human rights, and fights for genuinely
humanitarian relations between people: 'For us this stand is in-
separably connected with Cardinal Wojtyla, who in a way became
a symbol of all those trying to retain human dignity.'

One of the leading Marxist dissenters in Poland regards Wojtyla
as a reliable friend and protector of independent intellectuals and
students: 'He is an authority for them.' And a leading Catholic intellectual concludes. 'The Church is the only opposition in this
country. It acts as spokesman for the whole of society, it is the only
ideological alternative and the biggest liberating force.'

In June 1978 Cardinal Wojtyla expressed disappointment that
recent talks between Church and State conducted at the highest
level (including Gierek's audience with Paul VI) had not yielded the
results expected. Preaching in the presence of Archbishop Poggi,
the Vatican's travelling Nuncio, he raised the crucial problem of
recognition of the Church's legal status in Poland:

In the organized international or national community, the Church has
its legal status. On this basis the Holy See must, through its representative, ask just what is the legal status of the Church in Poland, however
much the question may surprise us, since we have always taken the factual
status of the Church in Poland for granted.

Nevertheless we pray now with our guest from the Holy See that the
status of the Church in Poland be clearly and legally defined. Because
being such a large community, a community almost as large as the
nation itself, the Church cannot be outside the categories of the law.
These categories must be absolutely clear. The legal definition of the
Church is at the same time a definition of our place, of all our transactions,
of all that which has its origins in the idea of the right to freedom of
worship, a right recognized throughout the world and set down in
numerous international documents.

All this lies in the answer to the question: what is the legal status
of the Church in our country? The question is a just and proper one.
For in asking it we can give confidence to believers, a guarantee –

which incidentally has often been given – that they are no longer to be categorized as second-class citizens!

The last statement Cardinal Wojtyla wrote before going to Rome for the historic conclave was on the occasion of the sixtieth anniversary of Poland's independence, proclaimed on 11 November 1918. This document was accepted without any changes by the Polish Episcopate and read in churches as a statement of the bishops:

Respect for all our rights of nationhood and territorial integrity is and must remain the foundation stone for international peace on the European continent ... By recalling the sixtieth anniversary of the restoration of our independence all Poles living today are duty bound to deepen and to strengthen their responsibilities for the common good of our nation. We cannot by our mistakes and shortcomings weaken or jeopardize all that which had been rebuilt with such difficulty at the beginning of the century. The responsibility for Poland's freedom and sovereignty resides with those people who wield authority in our homeland. Conditions should be created for society which would allow the whole nation to feel that it is fully master in its own homeland, on its own soil – which was granted us so many centuries ago by the Father of all nations. Great efforts must also be made to conquer the numerous internal threats, above all, those in the area of social, family and personal morality ...

We recall important historical moments and add to them a prayer of thanksgiving to the Father of nations, thanking Him for retrieving for us our freedom to live and exist in our own homeland.

Christianity in the World Many of Wojtyla's reactions to events in Poland, as reflected in his sermons, had a much wider significance. His assessments could equally well be applied to similar situations in the world, particularly in the context of human rights, and of relations between spiritual and temporal powers.

In some of his lectures, books and sermons he dealt with specific problems of the contemporary world and the universal Church. In his first book, *Love and Responsibility* (1960), his theme is marriage, birth control, abortion and love, both sexual and spiritual, between man and woman. The main contemporary interest of the book is that it deals with an issue which in the last ten years or so has deeply divided the worldwide Catholic community. The controversy came into sharp focus with the publication in 1968 of Pope Paul VI's encyclical '*Humanae Vitae*', which, contrary to wide expectations, confirmed the Church's ban on so-called artificial means of contraception as opposed to the so-called natural method based on the woman's monthly rhythm of ovulation. A number of subsequent episcopal statements in various countries attempted to defuse the issue by stating, broadly speaking, that while the ban remains binding in principle, in actual practice the use or non-use of artificial contraceptives is a matter of the individual conscience.

However, it would be wrong to judge the book only from this point of view. It is a very thorough study of human sexuality in general and of the problems of marriage in particular. While it is mainly pastoral in design, it sets the issues in a unified philosophical and theological context centred on the concept of the human person. Wojtyla argues that human love is above all an interpersonal phenomenon, and so must never be allowed to sink below the personal level to the merely biological or physiological. It is not merely sexual but also spiritual, and as such it is not limited to the bodily relationship of man and woman in marriage, but extends horizontally to other people – the children in the first place – and vertically to God as a Person. This is the responsibility inevitably entailed by true human love.

On the other hand the book does not ignore the bodily reality of man and woman, and goes into considerable detail in describing both the physiology and psychology of sex (the latter often with a great deal of insight that might seem surprising in an author who is now, after all, a celibate clergyman). The author insists that sexuality is operative not only in intercourse but also in apparently non-sexual relations, such as friendship, and also in freely chosen celibacy. The overall point is that, notwithstanding the law-of-nature character of bodily processes, they are to a large degree controllable by the human person. This field too comes under the sway of human responsibility.

All this may seem to be no more than a justification of traditional Catholic sexual and marital ethics in terms of a thoroughgoing personalism. This seems indeed to be expressly the author's aim. On two points, however, Wojtyla appears to go beyond the teaching current at the time of writing, and anticipates the insights of the Second Vatican Council. Whereas traditional teaching stressed procreation as the first and overriding purpose of marriage, both Bishop Wojtyla (as he was then) and the Council put conjugal love on a par with procreation, and both clearly refuse to establish, as it were, a hierarchy of marital aims. As regards procreation itself, the Second

Vatican Council also refused to reiterate the specific ban of earlier Popes on artificial contraception, while confirming the absolute prohibition of abortion and infanticide. Bishop Wojtyla naturally stresses the ban on artificial means of contraception which was in full force at the time of writing, but he puts almost equal stress on the inadmissibility of prolonged avoidance of offspring by the so-called natural methods.

The controversial distinction between lawful and unlawful means of family limitation, so clearly maintained both in the '*Casti Connubii*' of Pope Pius XI and the '*Humanae Vitae*' of Paul VI, is thus considerably blurred. The author of *Love and Responsibility* appears to be much more in line with the position taken by the Fathers of the Second Vatican Council and also with the majority report of the subsequent papal commission on Christian marriage. This report, while denouncing what it called a 'contraceptive mentality', allowed that responsible parenthood may entail limiting the number of children by any lawful means, which do not exclude contraceptives.

The book was published in 1960 and then slightly revised in a later edition at the suggestion of Fr Bednarski, now a professor at the Angelicum University in Rome, who was Wojtyla's superior in Lublin University in the Fifties. Further revision might be necessary, according to sources in Rome who know the current thinking of the new Pope.

As we have seen, Wojtyla enthusiastically embraced the decisions of the Second Vatican Council and insisted on their full implementation in letter as well as in spirit. Speaking during the Polish Episcopate's visit to West Germany in September 1978, at a reception given by Cardinal Hoeffner, Wojtyla succinctly outlined the post-Vatican mission of the Church:

We live in an era of fast development of the Church as well as of human and international relations, which at the same time are undergoing deep changes. In the Church this development was initiated by the Second Vatican Council. The mission of the Church, the evangelical mission of truth and love, places itself, as it were, at the very centre of the difficulties, dangers and contradictions which have grown up in the great human family as a result of multi-directional modern development. The Church has launched herself on the path of a permanent *aggiornamento* which means taking a new look not only at our present but also at our past, our history. We look at the history of the Church and the history of our peoples from the point of view of our common 'beginnings', and this implies a return to the very sources of Christian truth and our evangelical mission.

In his book *The Foundations of Renewal*, a study of the implementation of the Second Vatican Council (published in 1975), Wojtyla analysed the problem of dialogue, a concept central to the Catholic Church's attitude to the world, and to her relations with other Christian churches, non-Christian religions and non-believers. In particular the author dealt with the relationship between faith and dialogue.

Wojtyla defines faith not as intellectual assent to a set of dogmatic propositions but rather as a state of mind and attitude on the part of the believer. Faith is an overall act and a permanent predisposition which informs particular actions, but as such it is also a conscious response to God as He has revealed Himself to mankind. Faith so understood – it is argued – is perfectly compatible with dialogue.

The basic test here is a quotation from the Council's Declaration on Religious Freedom:

Truth ... is to be sought after a manner proper to the dignity of the human person and his social nature. The inquiry is to be free, carried on with the aid of teaching or instruction, communication and dialogue. In the course of these, men explain to one another the truth they have discovered, or think they have discovered, in order thus to assist one another in the quest of truth. Moreover, as the truth is discovered, it is by a personal assent that men are to adhere to it.

Within this assent, writes the cardinal, there is room for further search and for the enrichment of the faith. The Council has accepted dialogue as a means of enriching the faith, precisely through 'communication', i.e. exchange of thoughts. The author contrasts this with an earlier attitude in the Church which, in the interest of the purity of the faith, instead favoured separation from others 'who believe differently', or non-believers. Dialogue so conceived has nothing in common with religious indifferentism. On the contrary, it is an active concern for truth and other people's relation to the truth which, by virtue of their humanity, they are obliged to seek.

This, however, implies absolute respect for the convictions of others and the human conscience. 'This sacred Synod ... professes its belief that it is upon the human conscience that these obligations fall and exert their binding force. The truth cannot impose itself except by virtue of its own truth, as it makes its quiet but powerful entrance into the mind.' Thus the Council in its Declaration on Non-Christian Religions calls upon the faithful to 'acknowledge, preserve and promote the spiritual and moral goods among these men of other religions as well as the values in their society and culture', stressing at the same time that such respectful discernment is laid down by Christian teaching.

Even more formulations of this kind are to be found in the Decree on Ecumenism, which treats on relations with other Christian denominations, and to which a separate chapter is devoted in the book. The situation of dialogue is for Catholics a test of the maturity of their faith, which at the same time is a test of their love for people whose convictions are different from theirs.

This is a difficult test from which, however, no member of the Church can be exempted, according to Wojtyla. How difficult it is becomes clear when we scan those Council documents which deal expressly with unbelief and atheism. The Constitution on the Church in the Modern World points out that whereas:

... those who wilfully shut out God from their hearts ... are not free of blame, believers themselves frequently bear some responsibility for this situation. For taken as a whole, atheism is not a spontaneous development but stems from a variety of causes, including a critical reaction against religious beliefs, in some places against the Christian religion in particular. Hence believers can have more than a little to do with the birth of atheism.

Here, comments Cardinal Wojtyla, the proper function of dialogue and its relation to faith becomes particularly evident. It is a means of enriching the faith and a test of love towards other men undertaken on the ground of that faith.

Wojtyla has shown himself in no way accommodating towards atheism. But he has frequently insisted on the complex nature of the whole subject of atheism, which can either be imposed by a political system or just come about as a matter of personal choice. The cardinal analysed the psychological condition of an atheist:

We should consider this human being in the light of faith, and therefore, as an object of God's will of salvation. The loneliness of an atheist, who neither believes nor hopes for life beyond the present, pushes his desire of immortality towards collectivism. One could well ask whether collectivism gave us atheism or vice versa, or whether atheism favours collectivism. It is necessary to demonstrate to an atheist that religion is not an alienation from the world, but a conversion to God. This is quite a different thing, because God does not ask us to withdraw from this world.

A dialogue with atheists is therefore absolutely necessary. 'He has a profound knowledge of the theory and practice of atheism, and knows how to face it,' said Cardinal König, Archbishop of Vienna. The Church must cease to be silent and begin to speak, and that is precisely what the Church did through the Council and then the Synods of Bishops. It is very important to realize, Wojtyla once preached, in what measure and in what way the reinterpretation of the Gospel opens new ways for the teaching. Christians have a duty to 'shape the face of the earth' and to 'make human life more human. It is their duty to give so-called social progress the right meaning.' It is also wrong, said Wojtyla on another occasion, to 'consider Christian ethics as being concerned only with the personal life of individuals, and socialist ethics as being concerned with social virtues. Christian ethics is not merely a programme of individual morality but contains in its fundamental assumptions a programme of social morality.'

Of course ecumenism comes within the terms of a dialogue as well. Just four days before Wojtyla's election the Protestant Billy Graham preached to an overflow audience at St Anne's Catholic church in Krakow, at the personal invitation of Cardinal Wojtyla. The ecumenical cause is great and difficult, as Wojtyla sees it. It does not seem possible for him that there should still remain the drama of division among Christians – a cause of confusion and perhaps even of scandal. He wants to proceed along the way already begun, by favouring those steps which serve to remove obstacles.

In saying that he would pursue ecumenism 'without compromise but without hesitation', John Paul I had meant a return to Pope John XXIII's fearless desire to have charity at the base of the return to Christian unity, rather than the theological approach (as during Paul VI's pontificate). Cardinal Wojtyla extends the idea of charity to all mankind, but the road is long and difficult, as he clearly said in one of his sermons in January 1978.

The theme of the sermon were the words of St Paul that 'our hope cannot deceive us'. Modern man tends to strive only for what he considers practicable and achievable. This is too easy. The mark of the Christian is to strive for things that are above his human possibilities and to 'hope against hope'. For hope, of course, is not a human virtue. It is one of the divine virtues, and can be maintained only by the grace of God, through cooperation with that grace. The classic example of the impracticable is Christ's command to love our enemies:

And here the classic example is Christ himself, whose life, humanly speaking, ended in disaster. And yet He was victorious. Such hope is also the driving force of the movement towards Christian unity. The obstacles along this way are daunting and discouraging, but hope commands us to go on against hope towards the fulfilment of Christ's prayer 'that they may be one'.

Much has already changed for the better, particularly since the Vatican Council. The very fact that Christians today increasingly stress all that unites them, instead of what divides them, is encouraging. However, progress is not as easy and as fast as it seemed to many in the first years of the movement. Some people thought that Christian unity could be achieved in matters of days. When this did not happen they lost heart. But the Church and our Separated Brethren do go on, conscious that the many differences that have grown up over the ages cannot be overcome in a few years. This requires a great deal of humility and love. At least we have learned to respect each other, and we continue in an atmosphere of religious freedom. But it may well be that instrumental in the achievement of unity will be our weaknesses, rather than our strength. It may be that we shall have to experience a real defeat and great sufferings, and these will reveal to us one day that in fact we are one. That may be so in order that we might say with conviction that unity was not our achievement, but God's.

The 'dignity of man', the basic measure of a human being, and the 'struggle for man' remain the main themes of Wojtyla's scholarly pursuits. But what is this 'Man'? The cardinal answers the question, yet leaves some more questions, at the end of his sermon in May 1978:

Man must discover himself, must completely rebuild himself, must completely redeem himself! Because Man is not just a piece of matter, like coal or a block of stone, nor is he to be compared to the finest statue. Man is an image of his God – God made him unto His own likeness! Man redeems and discovers himself when he steps into this image; when he discovers his own likeness to God.

Man cannot thus be tailored to fit some programme nor even some philosophy! Man, who was created to labour, was also created for humanity. ... Labour comes into the equation of progress only to the extent to which it serves the development of humanity, while a condition for this very development of humanity is Man's labour. And yet, Man's humanity develops through truth and through love.

... Let us ask ourselves if too much human energy is not being allowed to waste away; if new generations are not being endangered by frustration, by feelings of pointlessness towards life and towards work.

Do not set up social or economic systems, nor political ones, in which a man has to surrender to others the very thing that makes him what he is. Do not make him dependent on others, nor restrict him simply because he is a believer!

The word 'culture' is, in Wojtyla's vocabulary, one of those words most closely associated with 'Man'; one which defines his earthly existence and points to his very being. In October 1964 he said:

It is Man who creates culture, needs culture, and develops through his culture. Culture is an acquisition of facts by the exclusive means of which Man expresses himself. He expresses himself for himself and for others. The products of culture, which outlast Man himself, are a testimony to him. They are a testimony to his spiritual life, for the spirit of Mankind not only lives through its mastery over things material but also lives within itself, through themes to which only it has access and which only it can understand. It lives thus through truth, goodness and beauty – and can express this inner life without, and is able to objectify its actions. And that too is why Man, as the creator of culture, bestows an especial testimony on Mankind.

... Clearly, for over two thousand years of its existence Christianity has been a great source of cultural inspiration. What we must ensure is that this same inspiration can be discerned in the events of our own times as well as in the years to come.

The danger of alienation and the 'struggle for man' between the Church and Marxism came out clearly in Cardinal Wojtyla's address in Mainz on 23 June 1977 when he received an honorary doctor's degree from the Department of Catholic Theology at Johannes Gutenberg University. The reason for this honorary degree was, incidentally, stated as follows:

Because Cardinal Wojtyla has demonstrated new methodological paths for the Christian ethic through a phenomenological foundation and continuation of Christian personalism, and because he has convincingly portrayed the inviolable dignity of Man in an original demonstration of philosophical-theological anthropology, thereby making a very admirable contribution to the present moral-theological discussion on norm theory and basic values and winning great honour for himself.

In his address Cardinal Wojtyla said:

The understanding of the human being in his total richness, the understanding of the human being as a personal subject who is capable of self-determination on the basis of self-awareness, who wants to find his fulfilment in reference to the transcendental powers of his soul and who strives in different ways towards this goal, is the basic condition for a conscious and creative participation in the current 'struggle for man'. This struggle has been caused to a considerable extent by the concept of alienation. I am of the opinion that this concept, which is used in Marxism in various and not always contestable ways, does not have its significance in relation to the human being as an individual of the species 'homo' but to the human being as a personal subject. The human being, as an individual of the species, is and remains a human being without regard for any arrangement of circumstances. On the other hand, the human being as a person, as a personal subject, can in various circumstances be 'dehumanized', and he actually is and often to a high degree. He is robbed of his objectively inalienable rights. To a certain extent he is robbed of that which constitutes his human nature. All this is contained in the concept of alienation or is derived from this concept.

It is well known that according to the teachings of Marx and his disciples the human being is not only alienated by the system of private ownership, nor only by work in the system, nor only by the institutions which serve this system and above all, not only by the government itself. To this we can add that several of Marx's disciples, in Poland too, have become convinced – and have expressed this conviction – that the transformation of the social, economic and political system has not eliminated various types of alienation but rather has created several new types.

It is well known that Marx also looked upon religion as a source of alienation. The experiences of the human being who feels himself particularly duty-bound, in the context of the realization of Marxism, to think deeply about the problem of the human being as a personal subject, lead to the ever clearer realization that the only world of attainable and also of completely attained victory over human alienation is that very world which we find in the Gospel – and no other. Only in this world, in this dimension of understanding, reason and ethical sense of duty, does the human being find liberation from that which 'dehumanizes' him. And everything that 'deifies' him in this world certainly does not cause his dehumanization, since God's image is the basic measure of the human being.

I think that a special path for theology and for the Church in the contemporary world is opening in this direction, one which is emerging with all the tension of the growing 'struggle for man'. A special appeal is coming from this direction, an appeal which theology must not ignore.

Wojtyla is a man full of hope. When in 1976 he addressed the Harvard Divinity School in Boston on 'Participation or Alienation' he described alienation as a 'Marxist term'. He felt that there is a spiritual void created by Marxism, which he called 'the anti-catechism of the secular world'. After people satisfy their physical hungers, then what? Then it is possible, he thought, to 'fill the spiritual vacuum' of socialist nations with Christianity.

He returned to the subject of the 'dignity of man' and alienation in his Lenten sermons for Pope Paul VI and the cardinals in Rome in 1976. What really causes the final alienation, the spiritual degradation of man, is in Wojtyla's view an 'anti-love' that lies at the very root of all kinds of abuses of man by man namely:

His abuse by production, by consumption, by the State in various totalitarian and crypto-totalitarian countries, under various regimes which start with lofty humane declarations and end by violating elementary human rights. It is this anti-love that divides communities into classes, that incites nations and nationalities to fratricidal clashes, and splits the globe into oppositional 'worlds'.

Towards the end of this series of sermons, the cardinal was arguing:

There is undoubtedly in this world a great charge of faith and a considerable margin of liberty for the mission of the Church, although often it is only a matter of the margin. It is enough to observe the principal tendencies dominating the mass media; enough to pay attention to what is passed over in silence or what is said in a loud voice; enough to lend an ear to that which comes in for most opposition, to see that even where Christ is accepted there is opposition to Christ.

People want to mould Him, to adapt Him to their own dimensions and to the dimension of the men of the era of progress, and to the programme of modern civilization, which is a programme of consumerism and not of transcendental ends.

From this Wojtyla passed on to persecution as such:

One knows that countries still exist in which churches of all confessions are closed, in which a priest is condemned to death for the administration of baptism. Perhaps [here in Rome] in this one-time land of persecution, there are still traces of those ancient Christian catacombs and circuses into which the witnesses for Christ were thrown and torn to pieces by wild beasts.

Nevertheless, contemporary persecution typical of the last years of the twentieth century has a completely different context from ancient persecution, and its significance is totally different ...

We live in an epoch in which the whole world proclaims liberty of conscience and religious liberty, and in an epoch in which the struggle against religion, which is defined as 'the opium of the people', is carried out in such a way as to avoid as far as possible the creation of new martyrs. Thus the programme of the epoch is persecution, but to judge from outward appearances this persecution does not exist, and there is full religious liberty.

Moreover, this programme has succeeded in arousing in many the impression that it is on the side of Lazarus against the rich man, and, hence, on the same side as Christ Himself, although it is above all against Christ.

Can we really say 'above all'? We would like to be able to affirm the contrary. Unfortunately the facts show clearly that religious struggle exists and that this struggle is an untouchable dogma of the programme.

... It also seems that the means most necessary for the realization of this 'paradise on earth' are to be found in depriving men of the strength which they draw from Christ: this 'strength' in fact has been clearly condemned as weakness, unworthy of man. Unworthy and somewhat uncomfortable. The man who is strong in the strength given him by faith will not easily allow himself to be pushed into collective anonymity.

All this is an analysis of the 'Church versus Marxism' problem in the contemporary world as seen from the Christian point of view but by a man who himself has a profound knowledge of Marxism; by a philosopher and spiritual leader who has had to deal with practical political realities on a day-to-day basis. But Cardinal Wojtyla is a man of two worlds: schooled in a Communist-ruled country, he nevertheless belongs firmly to the West and its civilization. He knows that Europe, and the West which regards itself as Christian, is not the cradle of everything in the world. 'He has the necessary independence to be open to all sides. He knows the dangers of militant atheism, but he also knows the threat of materialism and secularism in the West. He will have something to say to both sides,' said Josef Homeyer, secretary of the West German Catholic Bishops' Conference. In 1977, Wojtyla wrote that Christ is a 'a reproach to the affluent, consumer society ... the great poverty of people, especially in the Third World, hunger, economic exploitation, colonialism; ... all these signify an opposition to Christ by the powerful'.

As a churchman in Poland Wojtyla created a specific image of a teacher and servant on the pastoral scene, an image that has all but disappeared among the affluent communities in Western Europe and North America, but which best reveals the spirit of Christianity. The people who know him maintain that he has little in common with those who use Christianity to give a spiritual veneer to a materialist and exclusively consumerist capitalism, and still less with those who use the defence of Christian civilization as a pretext for the persecution of their fellow human beings. He has always seen his mission as one that brings comfort to the oppressed, not one that makes the oppressor feel comfortable. A Vatican official who knows him well says that he always wanted the Church to concentrate on those Christians who live under oppressive regimes. By constantly emphasizing the need to ensure fundamental human rights and freedoms for all, he appeared to endorse the politically active involvement of many Catholic missionaries, particularly in Africa, Asia and Latin America.

In Latin America, a Columbian theologian says, the Church is threatened by Fascism in the same way as it is threatened by Communism and atheism in Europe. The great theme at the moment is the 'theology of liberation', and a need for justice for the common people. Marxism and Communism, the abandonment of pluralism, are part of the machinery of this theology. These ingredients Wojtyla knows only too well from the inside. 'He is in a position to fight for the Catholic Church in countries with dictatorial regimes. His nationality gave much solidity to the Church,' said Carmine Rocco, Papal Nuncio to Argentina.

Cardinal Wojtyla's main preoccupation has always been how to make an effective contribution to the cause of permanent and prevailing peace, of the development of international justice, both in his country and in the world at large. To ensure human progress and ease, leaders and governments must cooperate more closely with their citizens. The Church will always help. One thing is certain: that there cannot be real human progress and durable peace without a courageous, loyal and unselfish search for cooperation and unity among all people.

Wojtyla has always tried to exercise a gentle, moderating influence in the spirit of the Encyclical '*Pacem in Terris*'. The encyclical envisaged a wide area in which Catholics could meet and come to an understanding both with Christians of other churches and with non-Christians who were endowed with the light of reason and with a natural and imperative honesty. One must never confuse error and the person who errs, the encyclical tells us. Such a person must be treated in accordance with his dignity as a human being. There must be no compromise in matters of religion and morals, but even movements antagonistic in these matters may contain positive elements, deserving approval.

For Wojtyla the encyclical *'Pacem in Terris'* has proved remarkably prophetic in pinpointing two of the factors which have come to the fore in peacemaking in the past decade or so: the direct connection between peace and the observance of human rights, and the question of justice for the poor and the oppressed. In other words no real peace could be achieved without justice for all, and respect of human rights by those in power. This conclusion clearly appears in everything that Wojtyla has said and done over the years.

Finally he sees in the Papacy a single unifying factor in the world. In his pastoral letter to the young people of Krakow at the beginning of the academic year on 3 October 1978, Cardinal Wojtyla wrote:

It was significant that both the funeral of the Holy Father Paul VI and the subsequent inauguration of the new pontificate of John Paul I were attended by representatives of about a hundred countries of East and West. Seeing this vast concourse and being aware of the many political and ideological divisions in the modern world, one could not help thinking that the person and office of the Holy Father in some way tends to unite these people around himself, even to reconcile them, notwithstanding all their differences, even their mutual struggles.

7
Wojtyla the Man

'A down-to-earth individual who has time for everybody; everybody knew Cardinal Wojtyla ...'

'He's got an ease and openness in his dealings with people, especially young people ...'

'The young and the intellectuals see him as an excellent raconteur, a partner, a father ...'

'A man of God ... conciliatory and full of good sense ...'

'He has an absolute radiant personality ...'

'A younger John XXIII full of sunny optimism ...'

These are impressions of Wojtyla as expressed by friends, colleagues, teachers and students. What sort of man is he?

He has the build of an athlete. His rugged, sturdy, 5′ 10″ frame, craggy eyebrows, broad-cheekboned Slav features and athletic posture suggest the toughness of a boxer or rugby forward. He radiates self-confidence, authority, and the uncompromising moral and physical strength of a provider. Suffering, endurance and hardship can be seen in his face. Yet this severe face, often looking down as he walks slowly and deliberately, with his slight stoop, will light up the moment he sees a friend into a warm, welcoming smile. He has a gentle smile, but quiet strength is the most striking first impression that he gives. His two-armed embrace is all-enveloping. And his strong, virile, baritone voice announces a new refreshing presence. The difference between the present Pope and the late John Paul I is that while the latter was a mixture of compassion and gentleness, the former is a mixture of compassion and strength.

Some people have remarked that he looks like an Italian, one of the northern Italian races weaned on the wind and the snow of the Dolomites. With his clear eyes and apparent firmness he displays a certain military appearance, inherited no doubt from his father. He could almost be one of those blue-eyed colonels of the Italian

Alpine regiments who treated their men as their sons and heroically led them into victory in the face of great danger.

Wojtyla's toughness and build are not just apparent; real muscles hide behind the flowing robes of the Pope, formed in the grim labour of the quarry in his youth, and since strengthened regularly by his sporting activities. Skiing, mountain climbing, tennis, volley-ball, canoeing, swimming, skating and even cross-country running suggest a man dedicated to an almost oriental concept of keeping both the body as well as the spirit in a healthy state.

But the feature of the new Pope which most stands out in people's minds is the fact that he is a Pole, the inhabitant of a land about which most people know little save that its invasion by Germany started the Second World War. Of course the Pope is a Father to the whole of mankind, and as St Peter's successor his parish circum-scribes the entire globe. Yet for all that, John Paul II remains a Pole; he is steeped in the traditions of his homeland, its culture and its rich heritage. This is important not because it suggests a narrowness of outlook, but because this very Polishness is a guarantee of a uni-versal viewpoint. The Poles have always been an outward-looking race – history and circumstances have forced them to be so. In par-ticular, their special inclination has been towards the West. Although Wojtyla remains a Pole, he is more than just a Pole, he is a European deeply conscious of his links with the Mediterranean Christian culture. He is also a European whose broadness of intellect and experiences through journeys to other continents have given him the means of spiritually embracing the whole Catholic com-munity and the whole of mankind. Cardinal Etchegarray, Arch-bishop of Marseilles, who knows Wojtyla personally and has met him several times, described him as 'an intellectual who is on the best of terms with the intelligentsia, and a vigorous philospher. A great theologian, who follows closely the trends of modern religious thinking. He is very attentive to the aspirations of the modern world, but he is also firm where the doctrine of the Church is concerned.'

In addition to his European and world outlook, Wojtyla enjoys the enormous advantage of linguistic virtuosity when it comes to his international dealings and contacts. He is at home not only in Latin but in French, German, Spanish and, of course, Italian, which he speaks almost flawlessly. His almost indiscernible Polish accent is no more disturbing to the Romans than the Bergamasque of John

XXIII, the Brescian of Paul VI, or the endearing Veneto of John Paul I. He can read and even speak some other languages too.

The physical strength of the man is matched not only by immense inner moral strength but by a rare ability to put the convictions of his spirit into words and to deliver those words with the power and selective stress of a superb orator. It is one thing to stand in a pulpit and voice moral and theological platitudes to a dozing congregation, inflicting on them a penance of sorts. It is something else to be able to prepare your tests not with words that people necessarily want to hear but with words that must be said, and then to captivate the listeners, to hold them in your hand in a perfect intangible harmony. It is a feeling every actor loves and every demagogue abuses. Unless used with great discretion, it can be a most dangerous weapon. Wojtyla has this gift, and has been able to handle it carefully, never letting it slip out of control. He has always shown complete mastery of every situation, and control of the crowd in any circumstances.

His mastery over public relations is complete, and his sometimes uncanny instinct with the crowd places him apart from many other Church leaders. He creates an impression of hope and vigour, the combination of firmness and a power-sharing openness and warmth as he wins people's hearts. Behaving with the effortless confidence of one who knows exactly what he is doing, he reads his prepared texts without improvising, but his pauses, his moments for reflection and his sudden emphasis on a crucial phrase frequently say more than words alone.

His power to subconsciously elicit attention can be attributed to the actor in him, or the poet, yet what remains so impressive is the concentration which he brings to everything he undertakes. His sermons are direct and clear, often without much ecclesiastical terminology while the delivery is judged to win enthusiasm for the fundamental Truths he always seeks. After Wojtyla has finished speaking the crowds do not want to leave. Unless he is giving a sermon which is followed by the normal and sober continuation of the mass, he is in danger of being mobbed.

One of the stumbling blocks on the road to Christian unity has been the doctrine of Papal Infallibility, as degreed by the first Vatican Council (1869–70). The office of Pope was then seen as having been divinely instituted, while the power of the Pope spread over all areas of the universal church. Without explicitly denying the resolutions of the first Council, the Second Council made it clear that the Pope, though vested with ecclesiastical powers, should be regarded more as a teacher and a servant. In the words of Wojtyla: 'Make me a servant, the servant of servants.' Or, as Britain's Cardinal Hume said of the new Pope: 'He is likely to be a profound teacher ...'

The two nouns 'servant' and 'teacher' between them summarize all that is best in Christianity; they surely form the very nucleus of Christ's teaching. But bearing in mind the doctrine of Papal Infallibility, which is still on the Vatican's statute books, and consequently the likelihood that the teaching of the teacher no less than his service will be taken by many as being beyond dispute, what is Wojtyla's psychological profile? Within what sort of ecclesiastical framework does he function?

As the son of a strict and influential father, psychologists will tell us that his outlook is more likely to be a conservative, disciplined one. That much is true to some extent. It has been said of Wojtyla that he is traditional in doctrine and theology. But he is also a man of immense intellect and deep human compassion. He is a profoundly contemporary and worldly priest, with a feeling for the hardships of working people, and this made him the spokesman of a liberal policy on social issues who has shown himself on the side of moderate reforms in the sessions of the Vatican Council. Wojtyla is not afraid of the new. He does not have a catastrophic vision of the world. His mind remains open to everything that is new and good. He is a man on whom it seems impossible to attach conventional labels such as conservative or progressive.

Wojtyla has an extraordinarily strong religious conviction and deeply ingrained need for constant prayer. His deep spirituality is grounded in a burning and steadfast mind. Every problem he has ever faced, he has shared with God, in humility and in prayer. With his staunch and fervent faith, disarming sense of humour, charm and tact, a Protestant friend of Wojtyla's, who has known him for ten years, summarized him as 'a man whose soul is at leisure with itself'.

A priest recalls how as a young vicar he committed some serious misdemeanour and was strongly reprimanded by Cardinal Wojtyla. He was summoned for a long interview, after which the cardinal led him to the church to pray. Wojtyla himself knelt and prayed for so long that the vicar became impatient – his train was due to leave. Finally the cardinal stood up and asked the vicar for something that no priest can refuse: 'Will you hear my confession now?' The stunned vicar duly went into the confessional, and the cardinal confessed his sins before him.

Above all, Wojtyla is a thinker and a philosopher. His philosophy is built in no small measure on practical experience, and this in turn influences his actions. As a thinker he is a reflective and intelligent man with a searching, analytical mind, able to weigh up relative opportunities and dangers. He is relentless but he will not be hustled; he is brave enough to take his time in assessment.

Somebody who worked with Wojtyla for a number of years described him as an intellectual when in the company of intellectuals. 'As a real intellectual, however, he appreciated the value of simplicity. He was a simple man, in the best sense of the word, and was the same with everyone regardless of education, intellect, social standing or class. His simplicity in thought, deed and word drew him close to the widest possible range of people.' Reflective, and grasping the essence of a problem, he is concerned to be on the same wavelength with both the simple and the learned. He also has a rare talent for being able to undertake many mental activities simultaneously.

Wojtyla is thus an intellectual with a human face, who knows how to win not only the minds but also the hearts of people. This human, down-to-earth approach makes for ease of contact with his fellow man, but it would be a mistake to assume that Wojtyla relies on this directness alone to achieve results when the pressure is on. All who have observed him agree that the man is no pushover. He knows the art of Byzantine manœuvres and long-range tactics, having learned it in confrontation with a Communist bureaucracy at least as formidable as any bureaucracy in the world, and certainly as formidable as the Vatican's. He has the keen political temperament of a statesman who properly appreciates the many checks and balances in any situation.

When all normal channels failed, Wojtyla was somehow always able to find a roundabout way of achieving what he wanted. Once a parish priest in his Krakow archdiocese had to pay heavy taxes or go to prison. The priest had no money and asked the then archbishop of Krakow for advice. Wojtyla suggested that he should report to prison and 'pay the penalty'. But immediately the priest followed his suggestion, Wojtyla took over the parish himself as a simple parish priest, and told a thousands-strong crowd why he was there and what had happened. Within a few days the priest was released from prison, and life went on as before.

As a negotiator, Wojtyla will not be pushed to do anything, nor will he ever allow himself to be manipulated. He is a good listener whom few details escape, and although not self-assertive he will resolutely defend his views and the basic rights and freedoms of Mankind and the Church. His approach to any task is brisk and businesslike, yet with touches of humane inspiration likely to give nightmares to those steeped in protocol or with stuffy attitudes to procedure and methods. His way is to examine a problem from first principles and then see how they apply. An innovator himself, he is open to new ideas from others, though he is not inclined towards spontaneous changes or reverses. He is a man who has developed in a linear fashion, without sudden jumps or starts (except perhaps in his decision to drop Polish and take up the priesthood); he lives from the past, through the present and into the future all in a straight line.

Christ tells us the second most important commandment is 'Love thy neighbour.' That is precisely what Wojtyla does, though it must be a far from easy task at times if, as Sartre claims, hell is other people. The temptations of status and authority are many, not least in day-to-day contacts with subordinates who may misunderstand instructions or fail in any one of the tedious minutiae of administration. If in addition to status a man is equipped with intelligence and a sharp wit, without the necessary humanity to accompany them, then impatience is unavoidable and sarcasm not far off. It is to his credit that Wojtyla, while having both responsibility and intellect, has never subordinated the needs and worries of the individual to the needs and workings of the organization. He has always showed the greatest respect to people, regardless of their background, and has never spoken insultingly to anyone or about anyone, nor ever aimed his many stern pronouncements at individuals.

Everyone you speak to about Wojtyla will stress his humanity and sincerity. He is a man of powerful energy who knows his own mind. You could be sure of Wojtyla; you could trust him. His door was always open and you could talk to him in a free and frank way without diplomatic wiles or in fear of his reaction. He is a simple, straightforward man. This simplicity is not without a subconscious element of public relations, but this arises from his feelings, from what he experiences at a given moment. People who do not know him may come away with the impression of something akin to American-style electioneering. How wrong they are. It is all genuine.

Yet people who have contact with Wojtyla also notice that it can be difficult talking to him, partly because he poses multi-dimensional questions. One is thus unsure which particular sphere they relate to, and in answering him it is difficult to be sure whether one has hit the mark. This has also left the impression that he is a difficult person to get close to. He has never been overtly forth-coming in relationships, and has not easily established close friend-ships. Nevertheless, once those ties have been made he is unwaver-ing in his loyalty, which extends to every circle with which he has ever been associated; he does not forget people. Old acquaintances are never eroded by newer ones. He never forgets the old ones, and does not confine himself to the new ones alone. This is a remark-able loyalty, the more so since Wojtyla's rise has taken him from one end of society to the other, from the poverty of the stone quarry to the riches of the Vatican.

One of his oldest friends has this to say of Wojtyla: 'I liked him immensely; he was extremely sympathetic, likeable and had a ter-rific sense of humour. Yet, at the same time, he was the sort of person that one had to take seriously. I never felt embarrassed in his pre-sence, yet he radiated a certain charisma which stopped one behav-ing in a way one might well have adopted in the presence of others. For example, risqué jokes would be avoided in his presence.'

This charisma can almost be touched. Perhaps it lies in Wojtyla's eyes; they seem to radiate a rare humanity and goodness which can disarm you. When I saw him it was this penetrating benevolent look in Wojtyla's warmly smiling eyes for which I was unprepared. The only person to have looked at me that way was my late father. It was this quality that Cardinal Cody of Chicago was describing when he said that Wojtyla was 'a great philosopher and a great student, but a man down to earth. He makes you feel at home when you first meet him.'

Karol Wojtyla has been a poet, an actor, a promising student of drama and literature, a writer and a journalist, a labourer, member of a wartime conspiracy, skier, canoeist, swimmer, skater, climber, footballer, brilliant theologian and philosopher, priest, lecturer, professor, bishop, archbishop, cardinal and finally, Pope. What more could a man reasonably be expected to do by the time he reaches the age of 58? And yet there appears to be a significant omission. From what one can gather from the many available sermons, writings and speeches, from the memories of friends and colleagues, Wojtyla does not appear to have a scientific-technical dimension. The many pronouncements he has made on matters spiritual and ecclesiastical, but particularly on matters of faith, apparently contain few references to pure science and technology. Technology today is a runaway horse threatening to physically and spiritually drag Man towards his destruction. What is needed is a long overdue spiritual framework within which its fruits can be enjoyed but its excesses contained, while in the pure sciences a spiritual foundation must be clearly and decisively spelled out.

For all his success, Wojtyla is not ambitious. Some people who have known him for years feel pity for him in his new role. One person who knew him as a close friend in Krakow claims that he really did not want to be a cardinal, nor before that a bishop. He accepted the successive functions as the burden he must shoulder, like a cross, because this was God's will. All the others who have known Wojtyla for years feel pity for him in his new role, although as Poles they are proud and overjoyed. A man who would be close to the people, now he has to contend with bodyguards and protocol, and tries to escape them as often as possible. He is locked in another, vastly greater 'cage', like the one he complained of years before in his Metropolitan Curia ... A lover of nature, he is trapped now in the heart of a large European metropolis.

Cardinal Wyszynski referred to the new Pope in November 1978 as 'our highlander from Wadowice'. Wojtyla's birthplace lies in the foothills of the mountains, so strictly speaking he is not a highlander, but he has the highlander's strength and toughness, warmth of heart and openness. To quote Wyszynski:

He loves the freedom that belongs to a wanderer, adores his native forests and pastures and is enamoured with his royal city of Krakow – so enamoured in fact, that he weeps at the thought of his lost Garden of Eden and brings to mind the words of the Polish song: 'Oh Highlander, doesn't it grieve you to leave your native land?'

But the highlander from Wadowice, as he resides in the Vatican and, as in the same song,

'with his mind's eye at the native forests gazes
and from his cheek the falling tear erases...'

must surely reply: for Thee I do it, Lord. For God, for the Church,
its business and its enormous tasks which tower before mankind.

For Wojtyla the Polish Tatra mountains have a special fascination
which he once expressed in one of his sermons: 'For us the Tatras
mean a look upwards ... For us looking at the Tatras means looking
up at the heights ... For us this has an evangelical significance. The
Christian is somebody who looks upwards ... And the first person
who taught us to look upwards was the Mother of Christ.' For
John Paul II the world is bigger than Krakow, and the Vatican is
much, much higher than Wawel Castle, and even the Tatra
mountains.

Last Days before the Election   There is a general and significant con-
sensus of opinion both in Poland and in Italy, and in the Vatican
itself, that at the conclave on 26 August 1978 Cardinal Wojtyla received quite a substantial number of votes at one stage. A priest
who was close to him in the Krakow Metropolitan Curia says that
he came back extremely tense from the first conclave. Wojtyla left
immediately afterwards to do some mountain climbing, but this did
not ease his tension.

Only a few weeks earlier he was completely himself, just as the
people knew him during his reign in the archdiocese. On a hot
August day he was driven, modestly dressed, to lead a retreat in
the highland village of Ludzimierz and became very thirsty. The
driver stopped at a small modest cottage by the road. Wojtyla
knocked at the door, entered and found an old woman in bed. She
was ill and complained that everybody had left for the retreat, and
she could not, although she had wanted so much to see the cardinal.
Wojtyla had a cup of water, gave one to her, arranged her pillows,
then took a small holy picture out of his pocket, signed it and said
to the woman in a highland dialect: 'Here you are, mother. Don't
be sad. When your people come back tell them that you have seen
the cardinal face to face, and had a much better view than they had
from the crowd.'

Only Cardinal Wojtyla himself knows how he really felt between
those two conclaves. On 17 September, when John Paul I was still

alive, the cardinal, in a homily in Mogila, spoke gravely about the duties of a Pope:

The Papacy is a very high dignity, but also a very heavy cross ... The new Pope took upon himself the cross of modern man. The cross of the contemporary human family. The cross of all those tensions and dangers. The unimaginable danger of a new war which is always with us and in our minds. He also took the cross of all those tensions and dangers born of manifold injustices, violations of human rights, enslavement of peoples, new forms of colonial exploitation, the manifold sufferings of men and nations which only the Cross of Christ is able to overcome. For they can be overcome only through justice and love ...'

Quoting the nineteenth-century Polish poet Norwid, the cardinal said: 'You either follow yourself with the cross of the Saviour, or you have to follow the Saviour with your own cross.'

When the news came from Rome of the death of John Paul I, Cardinal Wojtyla was just celebrating mass in Wawel Castle Cathedral on the twentieth anniversary (28 September) of his consecration as a bishop. After hearing the news he locked himself up for three days and at the same time cleared a backlog of urgent and pending matters which required his attention. It was also then that Cardinal Colombo of Milan is on record as saying that the cardinals were prepared to elect a pope from anywhere in the world, as, for example, Cardinal Wojtyla from Poland ... Wojtyla was certainly tense, nervous and under a strain, according to his friend Turowicz, editor of *Tygodnik Powszechny*. Having been invited for a reception by some friends, he turned up, then excused himself minutes later saying that he was very upset. He must have expected something, Turowicz said.

With the cardinals of the world preparing to leave once again for Rome, Wojtyla's car too was waiting outside his residence in Krakow to take him to the airport. But this was the day when he was 'at home' to everybody who wanted to come to him for help or guidance. A very old and frail woman suddenly appeared, knowing nothing about what had happened. She was only concerned with one thing: some people living nearby had taken her beloved cat away from her. Could the cardinal help? Wojtyla put the old 'grandma' into his car, drove to the given address, retrieved the cat and returned it to her. Then he went off to the airport.

Arriving at Leonardo da Vinci airport in Rome he drove straight to the bier of John Paul I to pay his respects (as he did when he arrived for the funeral of Paul VI), and only then did he go to stay at the Polish College. The rector of the College recalls saying to Wojtyla, tongue in cheek: 'Well, who knows – maybe you this time?' Wojtyla laughed and said: 'Don't worry, it'll be an Italian.' However, two high officials of the Vatican Curia who had met Wojtyla more than once in Krakow told their friends on the eve of the election that a sensible world would want to see this man elected Pope. But naturally they thought, like everybody else, that this could never happen.

Then there was the last meal at the Polish College before the cardinal had to leave for the conclave. 'What's this?' he said in a bantering tone. 'Aren't we getting anything better?' The sisters had baked some sort of a cake, but there was no champagne because, as the rector said: 'As you are going, Father, we are all feeling sad.' Wojtyla replied: 'Well, let's say goodbye then.' He paid his respects to the sisters and shook hands with everyone. The rector said only: 'Cardinal, this will always be your home and we will always be waiting for you.' 'Don't worry,' he replied, 'I'll be back.'

Wojtyla was very concerned about the health of his friend Bishop Deskur, and visited him in hospital on the way to the conclave. Two days later he revisited Deskur . . . this time as Pope. And the world's reactions to the election must belong to the simple everyday people and the students. As an elderly woman on her way to mass in the very Polish American town of Hamtramck, Michigan, said: 'It's like having your parish become Pope!' While seven thousand kilometres away a young student girl said: 'We have gained a Pope, but here in Krakow we've lost a father . . .'

As the newly installed Pope Wojtyla walked down among the cheering people in St Peter's Square, the first to be greeted were some invalids sitting in their wheelchairs, then his driver and two other servants from the Archbishop's Palace in Krakow, who had come to Rome to see their old cardinal. Only afterwards, when the humble had been honoured, did Pope John Paul II formally greet the gathered heads of State, prime ministers and other official representatives.

8

The New Slav Pope

When dangers abound Almighty God,
Heaves on a great bell-rope,
And opens His throne,
To a new Slav Pope ...

His face will shine forth,
Like a lamp in the dark,
And lead growing generations,
To the light of God's ark ...

To support God's world,
Needs strength and hope,
So behold our brother,
The new Slav Pope ...

Just as nations turn to guns,
So love will be his arm,
And the Sacraments his power,
As the world lies in his palm ...

(Juliusz Slowacki, 1848, translated by Christopher Nowakowski)

Slowacki was one of Poland's three greatest romantic and 'prophetic' poets of the nineteenth century. True enough, a Polish cardinal was elected to the throne of Peter 130 years after the poem. And certainly dangers abound in the world.

The Catholic Church is in a period of transition, still shaken by internal and debilitating conflicts of opinion on many basic issues – moral, spiritual, social and even political. There, as anywhere else, the conflict between – to use the popular labels – conservative and liberal tendencies continues.

Not only the Church herself but the whole world is exposed to unprecedented tribulations. These are not confined to one country or even one part of the world alone. They are universal.

At their roots remains the crisis of man, who, in most cases, has lost his sense of the past and of the future, his sense of direction, and has to face a pervading materialism of one kind or another. The old institutions are falling or becoming less able to withstand various challenges. The new ones do not as yet grasp the whole dimension of the changes. At the root of these changes is the rapid technical and technological progress which does not leave human beings time enough to adapt themselves to changing circumstances. The fundamental question is: are the reformed or new institutions, both spiritual and material, relevant to the problems of the rising generation and the coming age? Are they speaking in an ancient language to a narrow and dwindling congregation, or looking beyond the horizon of present struggles to a different, wider and more hopeful world? Is there to be, within this range of problems, a confrontation or a sensible dialogue between Christianity and Marxism, including political Communism?

All over the world people long for security, human contact and mutual understanding. The Church, if properly guided, could bring back to many people a measure of internal stability, confidence in themselves and hope in their future.

The election of the Pope from Poland was greeted almost everywhere with joy bordering on euphoria. But expectations ride on the back of such euphoria. And here people should pause to ask not whether Karol Wojtyla is the man everyone says he is, but whether any man is capable of bearing the huge burden of expectations he now carries. If John Paul II arrived in Rome with a disadvantage, it is the sheer scale, the ideological and geographical spread, of the hopes which his extraordinary election has set loose. Or was it really as extraordinary and unpredictable as many commentators and experts have described it? Given the challenge in the contemporary world, and the many qualifications needed for a Pope in the latter part of the twentieth century – which Wojtyla can be seen to have – the election should have been predictable.

Nevertheless it was a brave and imaginative choice, one which displayed the resilience and universal character of the Church in concrete terms. And it provided a symbol of the apparent renewal of the Church, and its wish to express this sense of universality tangibly at a time when the institution itself is in the throes of a process of profound transformation. The election proved the Church's remarkable ability to survive and even flourish under hostile circumstances. 'The Church is the alternative State', said a Warsaw university professor. 'But, unlike the State [referring to Poland in this particular case], it works!' The Vatican, and even the world, is not a place where everybody is going to like the consequences of this election. One thing is certain – they will never be dull.

When John Paul II spoke to the crowd in St Peter's Square on the day of his installation, he ended on a note that reflects the striking changes that have taken place in the Papacy in the last two decades. 'Pray for me,' he said, 'and help me to be able to serve you.' His past pronouncements in Poland and in the Vatican, plus the fact that he assumed the name of John Paul, prove that he wants to devote all his efforts to the full implementation, both in letter and in spirit, of the decisions of the Vatican Council and the Synods of Bishops: the Church's discipline, collegiality in decision-taking, liturgy, missionary work, religious freedom, Christian Unity.

Pope John XXIII inaugurated the reinterpretation of the Papacy by demonstrating the power of simplicity, humility and charm, by calling the Vatican Council to adjust the Church better to the modern world. Paul VI continued this initiative. Pope John Paul I cast himself as a shepherd for all people. And now John Paul II is determined to follow boldly on the ideas set forth by the Council, even to go to new limits by being not only the servant 'presiding over the assembly of charity' but a teacher too. He deeply feels the need to go out into the world, preaching a message of hope and respect for human dignity.

Basil Cardinal Hume, Archbishop of Westminster, met Karol Wojtyla for the first time during the Synod of 1977 and at both Conclaves in 1978:

At our first meeting I was struck by the impression he gave of strength, determination and durability. Later, I came to appreciate his intellectual ability, his theological grasp and his evident love for his country and his people. He seemed to me to be a hard-headed but warm-hearted man.

As a pastor working in Poland, he has had to proclaim the Gospel and lead his people in practising Christianity under difficult, and sometimes actively hostile, political conditions. He has shown firm guidance, and yet patience in negotiations. He has maintained and strengthened their faith – which was evident in the response of the Polish people to his election as Pope John Paul II.

At the helm of the Vatican, John Paul II does not represent particular interests but is acting in the context of the universalism of the Church. Even as heads of the Church, Popes cannot separate themselves completely from their past, nor are they expected to do so. Their experience and personality exert a considerable influence on their decisions, helping to shape their policy. The 'indelible love' for Poland which Wojtyla proclaimed in his Papal address, provides fresh evidence of his approach to the new tasks, in the sense that the Church in Poland has emerged after over thirty years of Communist rule stronger than ever before, precisely because it refused to make ideological concessions. As the Paris paper *Le Monde* put it: '... in a world disunited, dominated by uncertainty, indifference and the most vulgar materialism, the Polish Church offers an astonishing example of good health. That Church is strong, well structured, and disciplined.' The London *Times* wrote: '... Polish Catholics have learnt that a Communist Party is not invincible; in the competition for the confidence and support of the people, it is the Church which has won and the Party which has lost.' The nature of Wojtyla's experience in Poland is likely to have convinced him that the traditions of the Church combined with unequivocal guidance to the faithful cannot be dispensed with.

All the 111 cardinals were certainly looking for a man who would be a spiritual leader with universal appeal as a personality and the ability to restore a sense of harmony, to speed up the renewal within the Church itself. But whatever denials might have been voiced, the political aspect of the choice cannot be completely eliminated. The Church, with its culture orientated westwards, is reasserting Eastern Europe's place in the civilization of the West, and by obvious implication condemning Soviet influence there as an alien force. The choice of a Pole draws attention to the unity of European culture, and the Soviet presence in Eastern Europe is shown even more to be an aberration imposed by force.

Poland itself has been put back on the world map more forcefully than for many years past. As Tadeusz Mazowiecki, a Catholic intellectual from Warsaw, writes:

There is suddenly a wave of interest for Poland in the world. On 16 October all lights were turned on Rome and on Poland. And Poland looked at herself. In this widespread spontaneous reaction we felt in ourselves an unusual upsurge of strength and hope. As if history had smiled on us. We are not used to that sort of thing. It is a significant turning-point in our psychology ... But in this self-reckoning there is no room for any sort of triumphalism. On the contrary, this historical moment imposes new obligations. We hope that it will not only strengthen our Catholicism, but help us to acquire a more universalist mentality and widen our perspectives. I think that a people that has given a Pope to the world must learn how to overcome its faults and ailments, it must show the world a religious spirit that is not only very much alive but binding and fruitful in everyday life. I hope, finally, that Polish Catholicism will show an unflinching solidarity with all men who aspire to a life of freedom and dignity.

But Poles remain realistic in the political sense. As they say in Warsaw these days: 'God is in heaven, the Vatican very far away, and Moscow just across the border.'

That brings us to the main political aspect of Wojtyla's election. He not only bridges the European cleavage but reminds the world that this cleavage is of recent origin. And so is the confrontation and/or dialogue between the Church on the one side and atheism and materialism on the other – a dialogue between Christians and Marxists. There is the ever-present danger of political Communism and therefore of totalitarianism. The degree of totalitarian regimes, both left- and right-wing, may vary, as indeed the aims of governments may vary, but the techniques of the oppression are very similar. And finally more secular and consumerist capitalism in the West presents a problem for the universal Church.

John Paul II proclaimed to the world his intention not to interfere in temporal politics, but at the same time he emphasized the Church's 'interest in and help for human issues, which must be promoted sometimes by direct intervention, but above all through the formation of conscience, to bringing a specific contribution to justice and peace on the international plane'. And he insisted that he will reach out 'to all who are oppressed by whatever injustices or discriminations, whether it has to do with economic, social or political life, or with freedom of conscience'. There is no promise here of political silence.

But here also is a man with first-hand knowledge of the religious policy of a Communist regime, who moreover has the intellectual ability to engage in a discussion about Marxism, but who at the same time is blessed with diplomatic skill, patience and endurance. He knows the real obstacles to Church–State detente and knows the value of the promises of the regimes involved. As Cardinal Wojtyla he was a party to an uneasy accommodation between Church and State in Poland because he realized that there is no point in a head-on collision, so he will not ask for more than he thinks essential to preserve spiritual freedom and human rights. A strong man but conciliatory, open-minded and flexible except on principles, he has always rejected compromise in essentials but accepted co-operation in practical matters. That is the spirit in which Cardinal Wojtyla, who understands the problems from the inside, negotiated for peace and justice for the faithful in his own country. In addition, he is likely to shift the centre of gravity of Catholic discussion away from theology towards the social doctrine of the Church, for he has had to present his people with a Christian alternative to the Marxist social gospel.

By his engaging personality and prodigious intelligence, John Paul II has caught the attention of the world and has created new interest in the Church, presenting at the same time a formidable challenge to the ideologies that compete for the souls of mankind, as suggested by the *Herald Tribune*. In what was once termed 'the battle of hearts and minds' it is the Soviet Union now, with its aged, rigid and conservative leadership, and ideological stagnation, which is on the defensive. Wojtyla's election underlined the resilience of Catholicism as the alternative repository of a universal doctrine based on Christian rather than Marxist values and traditions. When the Kremlin comes to choose its new leader – sooner rather than later – the members of the Party hierarchy in Moscow might well be hoping for a little divine guidance themselves. Whoever comes after Brezhnev, and this will be of paramount importance to the world, will have to face a comparatively young and shrewd expert on Communist problems and chances.

John Paul II is certainly the right Pope for the coming post-Brezhnev era. Christians in Eastern Europe will feel that their fight is worthwhile and their perseverance is important. What Stalin never understood, when at the Yalta conference he asked how many divisions the Pope had, was that given a man like Wojtyla the Church might not need any divisions at all. When the Church of Rome goes to Poland for a Pope, it is clear that something new or perhaps something very old is happening, and that the West is beginning to regain a sense of confidence.

John Paul II is a formidable philosopher who, as a result of hard thinking and difficult living, understands the great struggle of the century, the struggle between the totalitarian state and all rival allegiances. The time is ripe to have such a toughened intellectual as a Pope, writes an American commentator. Secular enthusiasms have lost their allure. Only very few still believe that 'the death of God' means the birth of an age of reason. Only the wilfully ignorant believe that a 'new man' is being shaped in the Soviet Union, Cambodia, China or Cuba. And the Papacy, that oldest Western institution, is more likely than any secular regime to enter its third millennium.

The election of the first Pope to come from a Communist-ruled country is a sign of hope for this most vital single factor in the life of some churches today: the dialogue with Communism and all forms of Marxism. That dialogue, in Latin America, where a third of the world's Catholics reside, and in countries like Italy and Spain, where many Catholics are allied to the Euro-Communists, could now enter a new and much more difficult stage. It was one thing for the Catholic Church, itself in the throes of development, to talk to Marxists undergoing a corresponding trend to pluralism and doctrinal openness. In that situation, Catholic and Marxist alike can search together for a totally new concept of society. It is quite another matter for the Church to find common ground with countries where the Communists are less flexible and are very far from feeling anything in common with the religious believer.

Wojtyla's election as Pope created a big stir in Italy. He is first of all the bishop of Rome and must therefore be acceptable to the Romans. He is an Italian Prince (the last of the pre-Risorgimento princes still on the throne after the fall of the House of Savoy), and wields great temporal power in Italy both directly and through the Christian Democratic Party. The majority of informed opinion saw the election as a great breakthrough underlining the universality of the Church and an opportunity for a relatively young Pope, with a lifetime of adult experience of standing up to Communism, to make the message of the Church once more an effective force. Contrary to expectations the crowds warmed to him and he enjoyed a popular appeal, especially to the young who matter most at this juncture.

In the Italian context the election raised the major issue of relations between the Church and the Italian 'Euro-Communist' Party. The Church has traditionally had a 'special relationship' with the long-ruling Christian Democrats, but the Vatican has nevertheless been moving forward, not towards the left nor the right, but

on its own steady course. Wojtyla knows the Communists intimately, and how much pluralism they can afford, if any. Besides,
he will find himself in the not unfamiliar situation of confronting
a Communist mayor in Rome. His experiences have enabled him
to understand better than most the similarities and the differences
between the Euro-Communists of Western Europe and their com-
rades in the East. He has shown willingness to maintain an open
dialogue provided that the Church's mission and vocation are recognized and the freedom to evangelize the nation is granted.

Latin America and other parts of the Third World may be
wondering whether John Paul II, so deeply involved in the struggles
of the first two worlds, will be able to understand the aspirations
of the third. No Pole can fail to understand aspirations to national
liberation, and Wojtyla has first-hand experience of the possibilities
and limitations of Marxist–nationalist cooperation, and of the
dangers of liberation leading to new forms of oppression.

The whole world considers the election of Wojtyla as a new initiative, a daring new experiment to break out of the old frameworks
and habits and to put the spiritual future of seven-hundred million
Catholics in the hands of a man who, the hope is, can quicken the
life of the Church with fresh ideas. With that choice, said *Le Monde*,
the Church has given proof of its vitality, imagination and creative
power.

This election marks a change of direction that will put 1978 into
the history books for another reason. The Papacy has never before
received such attention as an institution of significance to non-Catholics. The spiritual leadership of the Pope belongs to all those who
are 'transcendentally minded' – such has been the tone of comment
in the press all over the world – and the election of a non-Italian
has heightened the impression that the Papacy transcends deno-
minational allegiance. What is more, John Paul II's own personality
and convictions lead him to stretch out his hands to everybody,
Christians and non-Christians alike, and therefore he cannot but
enhance the office he has accepted. He is the Pope from the people,
with the people and for the people, whoever and wherever they are.
For the oppressed, persecuted, frightened and weary people of the
world can at last shout out 'Habemus Papam!' – '*We* have a Pope!'
If the meek are indeed ever to inherit the earth, then they will have
found their leader in John Paul II.

In the course of writing this book I naturally came into contact with many people of various nationalities who knew Wojtyla throughout most of his life. The one thing which they have in common is their total inability to come up with a single word of criticism, doubt, malice or suspicion about Karol Wojtyla. This must surely be a unique situation, for by the laws of probability alone one would suppose that each one of us has even inadvertently upset somebody at some time.

Of course the election of a new Pope is a time for joy, the more so in a strongly Catholic and nationalist country like Poland where a Pole becoming Pope is a hero, if not a saint, as far as the people at large are concerned, and as such must be all goodness.

The worst that I heard in Poland about Karol Wojtyla can be summarized as 'grudging respect' – and that from a top Communist official. Many people I discussed the new Pope with were not pious believers blinded by their faith and patriotism. They were cool-headed academics, intellectuals and officials, men of the world who did not rise to their present positions through naïve assessments of their fellow men. And yet it may still be argued that such was the euphoria prevailing among the Poles that men and women temporarily lost their critical faculties when it came to discussing Wojtyla.

I can only say that over the years in my work as a broadcaster, I have had a great deal of experience in interviewing people. I have spoken to rogues and to honest men: from government ministers and defecting secret-service heads to diplomats and managers; from university professors to editors and fellow journalists. I hope I can perceive the truth behind the words and distinguish between the fact and hearsay. It is a fact then, that the only 'damning' criticisms levelled against Wojtyla are that some of his sermons were too long and his written Polish too heavy and involved, and that sometimes he got impatient. I have felt it my duty to state all this, lest people reading this book conclude that men like Wojtyla exist only in stories of the lives of saints.